JULIUS CAESAR

and his Foul Friends

by Toby Brown

Illustrated by Clive

SCHOLASTIC

A division of Scholastic Ltd
London ~ New York ~ Toronto ~ Sydney ~ Auckland
Mexico City ~ New Delhi ~ Hong Kong

First published in the UK by Scholastic Ltd, 2006
This edition published 2012

Text © Toby Brown, 2006
Illustrations © Clive Goddard, 2006

All rights reserved

ISBN 978 1407 12414 8

Printed and bound by CPI Group (UK) Ltd, Coydon, CR0 4YY

2 4 6 8 10 9 7 5 3 1

INTRODUCTION

If you've heard of the Romans then you'll have heard of the most famous of them all: Julius Caesar.

But why was he the most famous Roman of all?

He was a great warrior.

He was stabbed in the back by his mates.

William Shakespeare wrote a play about him.

AND I COULD WRITE BETTER THAN THIS BARBARIAN BRITON AS WELL.

All of those things are true, but that's not the whole story. There's more to JC than back-stabbing and wars (although there are a lot of those). There's how he survived plots and pirates to become ancient Rome's most powerful man. How he soldiered his way to conquering lots of land, and how his death heralded the start of the Roman Empire. And, of course, there's how his love affair with Egypt's Queen Cleopatra changed history.

How do we know so much about Julius Caesar? Well, for starters, Roman writers wrote a lot about him because he was so important. But we also know about JC from a very unusual source – Julius Caesar himself. Among his many talents JC was also a writer. In fact he used to dictate to two secretaries at once. And, while he was with his armies, he did it on horseback as well!

In his writings (as in his life) JC always made himself look good, but there were others who didn't think JC was great at all.

If you want to find out why JC's friends turned against him, and if you want to know how he ended up like an ancient pincushion, keep reading. You'll get all the scandals in sandals from *All Hail Magazine*, all the political plots in *The Republican News* and all the best military tactics from JC's own *Military Manual*. And you'll read what the man himself thought in extracts from his secret diary...

It's a story of glory and a tale of treachery, so read on for the thriller of a lifetime...

THE YOUNG JC

ALL HAIL MAGAZINE
100 BC

Gaius Julius Caesar and his wife Aurelia are pleased to announce the birth of their son; also called Gaius Julius Caesar, or JC for short. We're tipping this baby to go all the way!

JC's family, the Julii, were one of Rome's oldest. On his father's side, JC could trace his ancestors all the way back to the birth of Rome. Beyond that they claimed to be descended from the Roman goddess Venus.

Despite having an impressive family tree, JC Senior hadn't been all that successful. He was a politician, and Roman noblemen were judged by their success in politics as much as they were by their success on the battlefield or in business. JC's father was well connected with some of Rome's leading men (after all, he came from a noble family), but he never quite made it himself.

In fact, the Julii family lived in an apartment block in a pretty run-down part of Rome. This may have been because JC Senior wanted to live among his voters, the ordinary people of Rome. But it's more likely that he couldn't afford a palatial villa for his family.

Several Roman historians tell us that JC had a very strict upbringing. Certainly being the child of such a noble Roman family was hard work. His parents (like all noble Roman parents) were ambitious for JC (although not as ambitious as he was himself). His family wanted him to serve the city of Rome and make a name for himself. As soon as he was old enough JC was sent to school to learn the kinds of subjects he'd need to follow his father into politics…

Caesar's schooldays

We know that JC was taught by a Greek tutor called Antonius Gnipho. Along with noble-born boys (and the occasional noble girl) JC would have started the day very early, walking to his class. There would be a brief break for lunch, then lessons would carry on until late afternoon. It was a very long day. Why was schooling so demanding? Well, there was a lot for children like JC to learn. Here's what his timetable might have looked like…

9

GNIPHO'S SCHOOL FOR NOBLE KIDS

TIME (HOURS AFTER SUN-UP)	SUBJECT	NOTES
I	ASTRONOMY	Teacher says that watching the stars can help you find out where you are (navigation) and when you are (time-keeping)... I say: I'm at school and it's very, very early.
II	DOUBLE GREEK	
III	"	The language of learning and culture... it's all Greek to me.
IV	PHILOSOPHY	How to use logic and reasoning to win an argument (it's less bloody than using soldiers).
V	HISTORY	All about the great Romans of the past (people like my uncle and my dad and eventually, me!.)
VI	DOUBLE MATHS	
VII	"	
VIII	DOUBLE LATIN	Reading and writing; all very important for a very important person (like me!.)
IX	"	
X	DOUBLE LAW	I've got to know the Laws so I can make 'em myself...
XI	"	
XII	PUBLIC SPEAKING	Very useful skill to have if you're going to be a leader of Rome...

cock-a-doodle-doo!

$$X + X = XX$$
$$X \times X = C$$
$$IV + VI = X$$
$$X \div V = II$$

ZZZZZZZz

As well as all those subjects, JC also had to learn more about Rome. He had to learn all about Rome's provinces, how it conquered more land and, of course, how it ruled them…

For several hundred years the Romans had been expanding their territories. They started by conquering their neighbours in Italy.

Then the Romans moved on to the rest of the Mediterranean.

By the time JC was a child, Rome ruled territory from Spain to Turkey and from Southern France to North Africa. These areas were organized into provinces, which were run by Roman officials. They raised taxes from the locals, took slaves from unruly tribes and recruited more soldiers as allies in new campaigns of conquest.

The legendary legions

Having learnt *where* Rome's territories were, JC also had to learn *how* they were conquered. For years the Roman army had proved itself the best in the world. They relied on strict discipline, tactics and good equipment to tackle the enemy. JC would have had to learn all about life in the legions. And, given his success on the battlefield in later years, it's clear that JC was a very good student. Perhaps he had a school scroll to keep notes on tactics and formations…

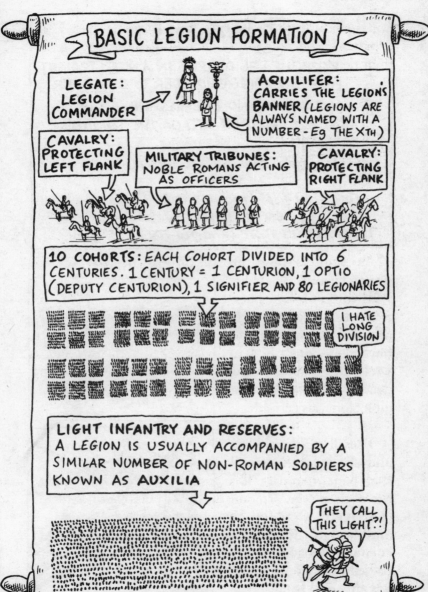

BASIC LEGION FORMATION

LEGATE: LEGION COMMANDER

AQUILIFER: CARRIES THE LEGION'S BANNER (LEGIONS ARE ALWAYS NAMED WITH A NUMBER - Eg THE XTH)

CAVALRY: PROTECTING LEFT FLANK

MILITARY TRIBUNES: NOBLE ROMANS ACTING AS OFFICERS

CAVALRY: PROTECTING RIGHT FLANK

10 COHORTS: EACH COHORT DIVIDED INTO 6 CENTURIES. 1 CENTURY = 1 CENTURION, 1 OPTIO (DEPUTY CENTURION), 1 SIGNIFIER AND 80 LEGIONARIES

I HATE LONG DIVISION

LIGHT INFANTRY AND RESERVES: A LEGION IS USUALLY ACCOMPANIED BY A SIMILAR NUMBER OF NON-ROMAN SOLDIERS KNOWN AS **AUXILIA**

THEY CALL THIS LIGHT?!

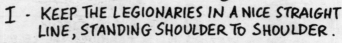

TACTICAL NOTES

I - KEEP THE LEGIONARIES IN A NICE STRAIGHT LINE, STANDING SHOULDER TO SHOULDER.

II - MAKE SURE NO ENEMIES CREEP UP FROM BEHIND OR ATTACK THE LEGION'S FLANKS.

III - ALWAYS LOOK AFTER MORALE.

One day I'll lead my own legions; then the world better watch out! There's loads more land for me to conquer!

As well as learning what a legion looked like, JC would have been trained as a legionary. He and his friends would have been taught how to wield the gladius – the deadly short sword that all legionaries carried.

They'd throw javelins and see how the metal shaft bent on impact. If it hit a shield or armour, the javelin would stick and weigh down the enemy, making him easier to kill as the legions advanced. Usually the

first thing the legions did in battle was greet their enemies with a hail of javelins.

They'd practise horse riding and build mock camps to learn all about siege warfare; how to take enemy camps, forts and towns.

In fact, JC learnt all the skills he'd need in later life, as a military commander and as a soldier himself.

The Roman republic

Rome had once been ruled by a king. But the Romans got tired of being ruled by one man so they threw the king out of the window (literally). The Romans wanted to vote for their rulers in a system called a republic. Sometimes unhappy citizens used troops to seize power. But these upheavals rarely lasted very long. For hundreds of years the republic of Rome had survived such disruption.

In JC's time it was considered very important to serve as an official of the republic. Men of JC's class expected to travel along what Romans called the Cursus Honorum or 'Racecourse of Honours'. Each stage represented an elected position. At school JC would have learnt all about the course that he himself would soon follow. He'd already be planning his own career…

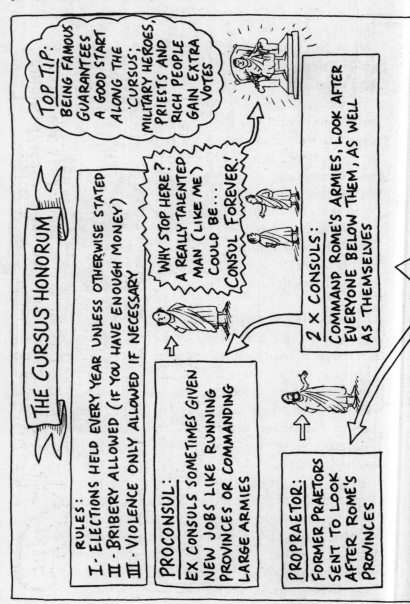

THE CURSUS HONORUM

RULES:
I - ELECTIONS HELD EVERY YEAR UNLESS OTHERWISE STATED
II - BRIBERY ALLOWED (IF YOU HAVE ENOUGH MONEY)
III - VIOLENCE ONLY ALLOWED IF NECESSARY

TOP TIP:
BEING FAMOUS GUARANTEES A GOOD START ALONG THE CURSUS; MILITARY HEROES, PRIESTS AND RICH PEOPLE GAIN EXTRA VOTES

WHY STOP HERE? A REALLY TALENTED MAN (LIKE ME) COULD BE... CONSUL FOREVER!

PROCONSUL:
EX CONSULS SOMETIMES GIVEN NEW JOBS LIKE RUNNING PROVINCES OR COMMANDING LARGE ARMIES

2 x CONSULS:
COMMAND ROME'S ARMIES, LOOK AFTER EVERYONE BELOW THEM, AS WELL AS THEMSELVES

PROPRAETOR:
FORMER PRAETORS SENT TO LOOK AFTER ROME'S PROVINCES

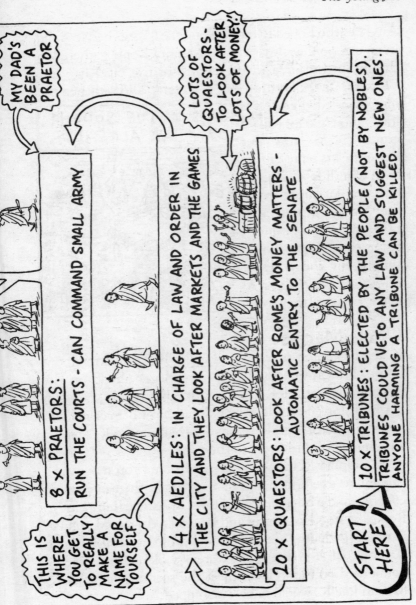

Anyone who hoped to move along the Cursus had to stand in an election. Each year the citizens of Rome gathered in the forum (an area in the centre of the city) to vote. Women, slaves and foreigners weren't allowed, but the men divided themselves into various groups (called committees) and put stones in jars representing each candidate. Richer citizens got more votes than poorer citizens and bribery was common. Rich candidates would simply buy the votes of the poorer citizens, just to make sure that they won.

Uncle Marius

JC learnt a lot at school, but he also had to learn a lot at home. Education could help a man get ahead on the treacherous path of Roman politics, but family was what got him started on the way. JC's father only ever made it as far as praetor, but there was another man in JC's family who made it all the way to the top...

JC's Uncle Marius was one of Rome's top men. As a general, he'd reformed the legions to make them even more effective and won an important war in Africa. Returning to Rome, he stood for consul and was elected a record number of times (including a stint of five continuous years between 104 and 101 BC). Using a mixture of violence and fame he dominated politics. He was just the sort of man a young Roman like JC would have worshipped...

JC's Secret Diary 87 BC Aged 12

I visited the forum today with Dad and Uncle Marius. It's an amazing place. On one side there's the senate house, full of Rome's great and good. Uncle Marius says that they're not allowed to propose laws, but they vote to pass them or stop them. The officials from the Cursus are the only ones who can propose laws. On the other side of the forum are the temples where the priests work. In the middle are the people. Uncle Marius says that they're the real power in Rome: keep them on side and you can't lose. That's why Rome's slogan is: Senatus Populusque Romanus: SPQR: 'The Senate and People of Rome.'

One day I want to be right at the heart of the forum, running the show...

Anyway, everyone was very polite to us. Well, they would be, wouldn't they? Only last week Uncle Marius and his friend

Cinna moved their soldiers into the city. They rounded up all their enemies and had them killed.

The trouble started last year, when Uncle Marius tried to get command of the legions fighting against Mithridates in Asia. It's a plum posting (and a great chance to rake in huge amounts of gold). The problem was that the new consul, a man called Sulla, had already been given the command by the senate. So, when Sulla left to go to war Marius and Cinna decided to march on Rome with their armies.

To make everything official, Uncle Marius is having himself and Cinna elected as consuls. Uncle Marius says they should win easily; everyone who would stand against them is either dead or away with Sulla. I suppose that's one way to deal with the opposition...

Taking advantage of Sulla's absence, Marius and Cinna had used force to overthrow his government. But before they could be elected as consuls Marius died, perhaps surprisingly, of natural causes...

A big year for JC

The next few years in Rome were relatively peaceful. But, in 85 BC, JC had more bad news. JC Senior died. The loss of Marius and his father could have seriously stunted JC's ambitions. But, luckily, JC's family still had friends in high places. In fact, JC was soon making his first waves on the political pond…

ALL HAIL MAGAZINE
85 BC

Things get easier for Julius Caesar!

She's been one of the most desirable women on the marriage market for years. But Cornelia Cinna, daughter of the current consul, has now been snapped up. Her father has given her hand in marriage to a young man called Julius Caesar. The husband-to-be recently lost his father (the praetor of the same name) and was facing a fraught financial future. In fact, JC was planning to marry a rich girl (from a dull family) but, as his mother told this magazine yesterday, 'Who can refuse a consul's kind offer?'

Double delight!
The young lady JC was previously engaged to, Cossutia, has been ditched.

NOW YOU CAE-SAR, NOW YOU DON'T!

To seal the deal, JC's new father-in-law, the consul Cornelius Cinna, has offered JC a favourable position in the priesthood. With a perfect wife and a bright future things just got a whole lot better for one Julius Caesar…

Gods and goats

The post in the priesthood that JC had been offered was one of many in Rome…

Forum fact: Roman religion. The Romans had lots of gods. These ranged from major gods like Jupiter (father of all gods) to minor ones like Forculus (god of doors). Priests led prayers and held the sacrifices and festivals in honour of the more important ones.

Keeping all the Roman gods happy was a full-time job, but priests often mixed their religious duties with political careers. Priests were at least as well known as some politicians, a fact that they could use to their advantage when standing for office along the Cursus Honorum.

For the young JC a position in the temple of Jupiter was a great start. But the post of *Flamen Dialis* was surrounded by all kinds of taboos. He would have to spend years studying before he could take up his post. Here are just some of the things a young priest had to put up with…

JUMPING JUPITER'S TOP TABOOS!

THE FLAMEN DIALIS CANNOT...

I: ...RIDE A HORSE

II: ...LOOK AT AN ARMY THAT IS READY FOR BATTLE

III: ...TOUCH OR MENTION ANY OF THE FOLLOWING: RAW MEAT, IVY, BEANS OR A FEMALE GOAT

IV: ...TAKE HIS UNDERPANTS OFF UNDER THE OPEN SKY

For the next three years JC was very busy. He was preparing to take up his new post and he had his first child, a daughter called Julia. She was to play a very important role in JC's future (as we'll see later on)...

Sulla the dictator

Unfortunately, things weren't going so well for JC's political career. His father-in-law, Cinna, was killed in a mutiny by his troops. With both Marius and Cinna dead Rome was open to their enemies. They had been members of what Romans called the Populares faction, one of two factions that dominated Roman politics...

Forum fact:

The Optimates: 'Rome should be ruled by the senate or rich and powerful people (like us)'.

(NOT ABOVE THE ODD
Vs ASSASSINATION/ BRIBE)

The Populares: 'Laws should help the poor and defend them against the rich...'

(NOT ABOVE USING RIOTS OR GANGS)...

Now things were turning against the Populares. As a blood relative of one Populares politician and son-in-law of another, JC decided to keep his head down...

Sure enough, Sulla, the leading Optimate, was still furious with Marius and Cinna. (It didn't matter that they were dead, he was furious with their supporters as well.) He quickly finished off the war against Mithridates (who was allowed to live) and left for home. Pretty soon Sulla was camped outside Rome with his legions. In 82 BC he stormed the city and had himself installed as dictator.

Forum fact: Dictator. In extreme emergencies Rome could appoint a dictator. Their rule would usually only last for six months. But without another consul to balance them the dictator could command all of Rome's armies and, in effect, had absolute power.

Sulla had great plans for Rome (mainly involving getting rid of his enemies and making his friends even more rich and powerful). One of his tactics was to publish lethal lists of names in the forum...

At first, Sulla seems to have tried being friendly to JC. After all, JC was young and he couldn't really help who he was related to. Perhaps, suggested Sulla, JC could divorce Cornelia and marry someone from a good, Optimate family instead. Everyone expected JC to abandon his wife and new child in order to save his own skin. They were amazed when JC didn't take the deal. In revenge Sulla refused to allow JC to take up his post as a priest in Jupiter's temple.

For a while it looked like the young Caesar was going to end up as an entry on Sulla's lists. For months he was forced into hiding. Luckily JC's mother still had some powerful friends in Rome. They begged Sulla to spare JC. Eventually the dictator agreed to let the young man go, saying:

25

LAW COURTS AND PIRATE PORTS

At only 19 years old JC had made a very powerful enemy in Sulla. Even if the dictator had shelved plans to have him killed, Rome was no longer safe for JC. Besides, he'd lost the post of *Flamen Dialis* and needed something else to do.

> **JC's Secret Diary 81 BC Aged 19**
>
> I hate to say it, but Sulla's actually done me a bit of a favour. All those rules at the temple were really holding me back. I mean, I could do without the goats and the ivy, even the beans, but not being able to look at an army? Or ride a horse? Or change my underwear? I'm sure I'll need all those things if I'm going to become the greatest Roman ever.

> *I think it's time for me to take a little trip to see the world. Maybe start making a name for myself away from the city. Frankly I'd rather be abroad when the next round of blood-letting happens in the capital...*

Soon JC was on his way to Asia Minor (modern-day Turkey) to act as an aide to the Roman governor. It was just what he needed. In Asia he built up his reputation. Sent as an envoy to Bythinia, JC became close friends with King Nicomedes III. A few years later Nicomedes left Bythinia to Rome in his will.

In 80 BC JC saw his first military action. The Greek island of Lesbos was occupied by forces loyal to King Mithridates. During a Roman raid on the island, JC saved the life of a Roman citizen. He was awarded a laurel wreath in honour of his bravery.

These adventures were all very well, but JC knew that the real seat of power was Rome. In between enjoying the hospitality of kings and the company of soldiers, JC was waiting for news from the city. In 80 BC Sulla resigned.

Officially he retired to write his memoirs; unofficially he threw wild parties and drank too much. Finally, in 79 BC, JC got the news he'd been waiting for:

REPUBLICAN NEWS
79 BC

Dictator dies, bugs blamed

Cornelius Sulla is dead. The fun-loving former dictator apparently attracted more than nobles and aristocracy to his cause. Doctors say he was covered in lice when he died.

I CAUGHT A BUG... OH NO...THOUSANDS OF THEM!

Some might not be sorry that Sulla's drawn his last breath (and his last list). But the Optimates of Rome still have a strong hand. Their enemies are exiled or dead, the courts are back in the hands of the aristocracy. The tribunes have been tamed and the senate is supreme. All in all, the aristo's champion did rich Rome a favour. Rumours that Sulla's opponents are planning to undo the dictator's deeds have been met with disbelief. Said one unnamed Optimate, 'The streets ran with blood before, and it could happen again, all right?'

When JC returned to the city he found it totally changed by Sulla's rule. The statues of Marius and Cinna had been removed and everywhere Sulla's men were in charge. There was no point fighting Sulla's thugs in the streets, so instead, JC decided to take his chances in the courts.

Courting popularity

Despite the fact that Sulla had reformed the courts in favour of his rich friends, a young and ambitious man like JC could still have an impact. Crowds of people watched the lawyers make their speeches. Particularly good speakers became firm favourites. It was a great way to be noticed by potential voters…

JC's first target was Dolabella. He was a former consul and was one of Sulla's most prominent supporters. He'd made plenty of money and there were persistent rumours that he'd got rich using illegal means.

JC spoke so well against Dolabella that his speech was published (unfortunately it hasn't survived). But Dolabella proved too powerful (and rich) for the 23-year-old lawyer.

JC wasn't put off by this defeat. At his next appearance he succeeded in proving that one of Sulla's friends had behaved terribly while serving in Greece. Unfortunately, the case went to an appeal…

These performances were certainly a good thing for JC's future career prospects but they also had a downside…

JC's Secret Diary 74 BC

Things are going really well. In the forum everyone knows the name Julius Caesar. It's a start, but frankly there are problems with all this fame. Sulla's supporters aren't that happy about being hauled up in court. It's not just that it costs them money to get them off the hook, it doesn't do their reputations any good either. No one's actually threatened me yet, but it's only a matter of time before they start wondering how to stop the glamorous, well-dressed, good-looking, silver-tongued, brilliant young lawyer (that's me). After all, they're all jealous of what a good lawyer I am and how famous I'm going to be...

Mind you, a good gambler knows to quit while he's ahead. I'd better be careful if I don't want my career to be too brief. Maybe it's time to take another break from Rome. Perhaps I should go and study abroad. After all, there's no point resting on one's laurels.

Rhodes scholar

The subject that JC was so keen to study (apart from how not to end up dead) was rhetoric. The art of using language persuasively, either in writing or in speeches was highly prized in Rome. They had learnt the skill from the ancient Greeks, and in Greece there were whole universities dedicated to coining a good phrase (as well as coining it in from the students).

The most famous of all the rhetoric schools was on the island of Rhodes. So JC set out to become a Rhodes scholar. The trip was not an easy one. Just off the coast of Greece, the island of Rhodes was often a target for pirates. Roman ships were highly prized...

JC's ship was captured and JC was kidnapped.

JC objected to the ransom figure, so the pirates increased it.

JC made himself at home while he waited for the ransom to be paid.

He even practised his rhetoric.

And he made them a promise.

Eventually JC's friends raised the 50 talents of gold the pirates (and JC) had demanded.

JC was absolutely true to his word. After his release he travelled to the nearest Roman port and commandeered a fleet of ships. He returned to where the pirates were anchored and captured them. JC then took them back to the Roman port and dumped them in prison.

The governor of the region recommended that JC hold the pirates for a return ransom. However, JC wasn't interested in money (he'd captured plenty of loot when he's seized the pirate ships). Instead, he decided to keep his promise. The pirates were all crucified…

Luckily for the pirates, JC was merciful. Instead of leaving them to die a painful death by crucifixion, he had their throats cut.

THE YOUNG POLITICIAN

After a year or so abroad JC felt it was safe to return to Rome. By 73 BC he'd been offered a senior post in the priesthood. (This time it was senior enough that he didn't have to worry about goats, ivy or underpants.) For the rest of his life JC would be one of the 15 people in Rome who organized the calendar, arranged festivals and oversaw all religious events. The position also gave him the power to reward friends. In fact, being a priest would be a very useful sideline for JC as he turned his thoughts to his political career…

JC's Secret Diary 71 BC

Finally, my first official political position! I'm a tribune in the military. It's my first step on the Cursus Honorum (and it won't be my last). Shame there's no serious wars for me to fight in. Mithridates is still alive somewhere in Asia but he's still licking his wounds, Pompey beat the rebels in Spain and then he came back to Italy to give Crassus a hand putting down a slave revolt led by that gladiator, Spartacus.

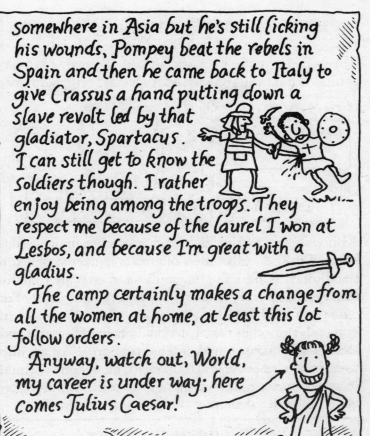

I can still get to know the soldiers though. I rather enjoy being among the troops. They respect me because of the laurel I won at Lesbos, and because I'm great with a gladius.

The camp certainly makes a change from all the women at home, at least this lot follow orders.

Anyway, watch out, World, my career is under way; here comes Julius Caesar!

At the start of Caesar's political career Crassus and Pompey were the consuls. At 36, Pompey had literally made a name for himself as a general.

YEAH, THAT'S RIGHT, I'M CALLED POMPEY THE **GREAT** NOW.

His fame (and name) won him the post of consul. His fame probably didn't help his relationship with Crassus, who never managed to copy Pompey's military genius. But Crassus had his own special political talents.

EVERYONE OWES ME MONEY!

Although the consuls had fought together under Sulla's banner, they'd both fallen out with the dictator. Now that Sulla was dead, the tide in Rome was turning against the Optimates and it was an excellent time for JC to start out as a politician.

JC's career really began to take off in 69 BC. He was elected as a quaestor and entered the senate for the first time. Instead of being sent to work in the treasury of Rome JC was being sent to count money in Spain. But just before he left JC suffered another two deaths in the family.

REPUBLICAN NEWS

69 BC

RIP, VIP says JC

There were sombre scenes at the forum yesterday as Julia, Marius' widow, was laid to rest. Recently, praising the name of Marius has been enough to get anyone on the wrong side of the Sulla squad (and earn an entry in their top ten targets). But that didn't stop the chief mourner, her nephew, Julius Caesar. The new quaestor gambled that now was the time to restore Marius' name to its rightful place in the forum.

When masks showing the dead general's face were carried in front of the funeral procession the poorer sections of the crowd erupted in cheers.

Gods and kings

Seeing that the crowd were on his side, Julius Caesar delivered a fantastic speech. He reminded everyone that his family are descended from the goddess Venus and the first kings of Rome. It was a fine bit of flowery speaking and was well received by the Populares in the crowd.

Within weeks JC had to lay on another funeral, this time for his wife, Cornelia. Despite his grief, he wasn't about to miss another opportunity to perform. This time JC used the funeral to celebrate the life of Cornelia's father, Cinna.

Marius and Cinna had been declared enemies of the state by Sulla. By celebrating their lives publicly JC was making his position clear. It was enough to earn him more enemies from the Optimate camp, so as soon as the funeral was over JC set off for his year in Spain.

Spanish holiday

Little is known about JC's year as a young quaestor in Spain but we do know he did a bit of sightseeing while he was there…

JC's Secret Diary 69 BC Cadiz

Had a day off yesterday and travelled to Cadiz and the temple of Hercules. There's a big statue of Alexander the Great. What a man. By the time he was my age he'd conquered all of Greece, the whole of Mesopotamia, and his armies had marched as far away as some place called India. He'd travelled thousands of miles, fought and beaten the armies of the world and sat at the head of a huge empire. What have I done? Counted money for the treasury, seen a bit of action in the Mediterranean and fought a few pirates. Hardly the stuff of legends, is it? No one will write histories about 'Julius Caesar the Taxman'...
Seeing the statue almost had me in tears.
To think, I've wasted my

great

> *life so far. It's time I started taking my place in the history books. I WILL be greater than Pompey, or Alexander, or anyone else for that matter. It's just a question of playing the game...*

By 66 BC JC was back in Rome and married again. This time his wife was Pompeia, granddaughter of Sulla himself. By marrying her, JC made it clear that he wasn't automatically against all of Sulla's relatives. The fact that she was well connected and rich probably didn't hurt.

Playing the game

When JC returned he found the Roman senate discussing the pirate problem. Rome needed someone to rid them of the sea-bound bandits. A motion was proposed giving Pompey a special command which could last up to three years. This was extremely rare and caused quite a fuss amongst the traditionalists, who preferred commands to only last a year. But JC spoke in favour of Pompey and the senate had to listen because...

It took Pompey just three months to suppress the pirates and soon he was looking for another command. Again JC was among those who supported his going east. There he could continue the war against Mithridates (who was once again threatening Roman possessions abroad). Backing Pompey made JC some powerful friends.

JC himself was appointed curator of the Appian Way. The road connected Rome with Italy's most important port at Brundisium, but it was in a terrible state. JC had to spend all his own money on maintenance. But such costs had their benefits for an ambitious politician...

Despite all the free advertising, paying for the roads put JC in massive debt and the next step along the Cursus Honorum would cost him even more money. Fortunately there was at least one man in Rome who was quite happy to lend money to an up-and-coming politician like Caesar...

JC's Secret Diary 67 BC

I went to see Crassus today about a loan. It seems I've spent everything I had (and a lot I didn't). He offered me favourable terms on a large sum of money. While I'm paying him back he can rely on my vote and my backing whenever he needs it. When he asked why he should back me I told him that I was a good investment; worth every penny. I told him straight: 'I'm buying my way along the Cursus Honorum'. Soon I'll be standing for the post of Aedile and that takes money. Not just to get elected but to do the job. I'm going to put on some of the greatest gladiator games ever seen in Rome...

In 66 BC JC was elected as aedile for the year. Elected alongside him was an Optimate candidate, Bibulus. He was everything that Julius Caesar was not. He was rich, conservative and unwilling to take risks. Bibulus spent the rest of his career being compared to JC. And JC outshone his colleague at every turn. For instance, when they organized gladiator games together, this is what happened...

WE ARE PROUD TO PRESENT:

320 GLADIATORS.

ALL WILL WEAR SILVER ARMOUR AND WILL FIGHT TO THE DEATH IN HONOUR OF GAIUS JULIUS CAESAR SENIOR WHO DIED 20 YEARS AGO.

TODAY'S GLORIOUS GLADIATOR GAMES ARE BROUGHT TO YOU BY:

JULIUS CAESAR, AEDILE, LOVING SON OF THE AFOREMENTIONED, AND WINNER OF THE CITIZEN'S CROWN AT LESBOS (AND MC BIBULUS THE OTHER AEDILE).

JC's games were so extravagant that before they the senate passed laws restricting the number of gladiators allowed into Rome to less than 320.

Although Bibulus shared the cost of the games he never seemed to get the credit for them. JC was proving to be an excellent politician and an even greater spender of Crassus' money. JC's was now a household name.

Soon he chalked up another great honour, getting himself elected as Pontifex Maximus (or chief priest)…

ALL HAIL MAGAZINE
ALL HAIL CAESAR SPECIAL 63 BC

Exclusive access to the home of Julius Caesar and his new wife Pompeia.

The young couple are enjoying the house which comes with JC's new lifetime post as Pontifex Maximus. Next door to the home of the vestal virgins and right on the forum, the address is one of the most sought after in all of Rome.

In a surprise move, the young JC beat stiff opposition to become chief of Rome's religious affairs. But JC himself was sure of victory. On the day of the election JC told his mother, Aurelia, that he'd 'either return home Pontifex Maximus or not at all.'

MAXIMUM LUXURY FOR PONTIFEX MAXIMUS

As his mother told this magazine, 'He always was a confident boy.'

The bald and the beautiful
And from these pictures you can see why…

Unlike other stuffy politicians, JC is always kitted out in the very best togas. He wears his senatorial threads loose, with the purple border fringed around the wrists. Rumour has it that he has all his body hair plucked, apart from what remains on his head. He needn't worry; the dashing Pontifex's bald spot is easily covered by the man's greatness. He almost always wears the laurel wreath he was awarded for action at Lesbos when he was a youth. 'Nature made me bald but Rome gave me the means to cover it up,' says our host. No need to cover up on our account, JC!

For the rest of his life JC would be Pontifex Maximus, Rome's most powerful priest. Of course, that didn't stop him wanting political glory as well. By now, JC's progress along the Cursus Honorum was unstoppable. In 63 BC he was also elected praetor for the following year. But the fight between the Optimates and the Populares was about to turn nasty. JC would need all his skill to stay out of it…

SCANDALS IN SANDALS

Cicero became consul in 63 BC. Famous for his way with words and his high opinion of himself Cicero was desperate to get in with the Optimates. When an opportunity came up, he seized it.

Cicero had defeated a man called Catiline in the elections. Catiline had been demanding things like giving land to peasants and giving help to the city's poor. This was exactly the sort of thing the Optimates did not want. Soon there were rumours that Catiline was plotting to raise an army and seize power.

Most of these rumours came from Cicero. According to him, Catiline's supporters sealed their oath of loyalty by 'eating the entrails of a small boy'. When asked how he knew this, Cicero said that one of the plotters had blabbed to his mistress. There was very little actual evidence, but that didn't stop Cicero. He had the conspirators arrested, but somehow allowed Catiline himself to escape the city.

In the senate JC spoke for mercy. His opposition was the leading Optimate senator, Cato. While Cato was speaking, JC was handed a note. Eager to suggest that JC was involved in the plot, Cato interrupted his speech to ask JC who the note was from. Unfortunately for Cato the note was from his half sister, Servilia, who also happened to be JC's mistress. Despite this embarrassment Cato swung the senate in favour of the death penalty.

So Cicero had Catiline's supporters strangled to death. Although the conspiracy had been stopped the leader of the plot was still at large in the Italian countryside. The Optimates were now in a very strong position. Anyone could be accused of being in league with the conspiracy, with dire consequences.

Again JC showed he wasn't afraid of the powerful (and murderous) group around Cicero. Instead he called on the senate to send for Pompey to restore order. The general was well respected and wouldn't let the Optimates pick on their opponents. But JC didn't bargain on how much the Optimates didn't want Pompey ruining their fun...

JC's Secret Diary 62 BC

Well, I knew they weren't going to vote for my motion to recall Pompey, but I didn't expect them to sack me! The Optimates, especially that catty Cato, ganged up on me and voted to withdraw my praetorship. They're trying to get my supporters to riot in the forum. Then they can accuse me of being in Catiline's pay and get rid of me. Well, I'm much too

clever for that. I just took off my ceremonial robes and quietly walked home. When people asked me what was going on I told them honestly: 'The senate has overturned the people's vote and kicked me out.' That got a lot of my supporters pretty steamed up. For a moment it looked like there would be violence, but I sent out a message from home asking the people not to riot on my behalf and appealing for calm.

With my dignified request for peace in the city, the senate look like a bunch of scoundrels whereas I look like a future consul (which I definitely am!).

By appearing to rise above the factions that were close to war in the city, JC won huge popular support. The senate was forced to give him back his job.

Clearly JC was already an incredibly skilful politician, able to turn even the worst situation to his advantage. But the next crisis was altogether more personal.

Dressed for scandal

There's nothing new about politicians being involved in grubby scandals. Over 2,000 years ago, JC found that his role in public life made his private life all the more interesting to the citizens of Rome.

Each year the women of Rome gathered at the house of the Pontifex Maximus to celebrate womanhood in a festival called Bona Dea. It's not known exactly what happened at the festival but one rule was strictly enforced: men were not allowed.

In 62 BC, JC's wife Pompeia was in charge of hosting the party at their house. All men (including JC) were removed from the house along with any statues or pictures of men. But this year something went very wrong...

ALL HAIL MAGAZINE

62 BC

CROSS-DRESSING CLODIUS CROSSES THE LINE

This year's sacred secret celebration of all things female has been the subject of sacrilege. Outrage swept through the women of Rome as a MAN was outed at the party. 'We couldn't believe it,' said one lovely lady, 'he was dressed as a woman but you could tell he was a man really.'

The offender was none other than Publius Clodius, an upper-class twit with a fondness for foolery (and a fondness for a certain Mrs JC if the gossip is to be believed). He stands accused of:
• Being a man.
• Bribing a maid to smuggle him in.
• Dressing like a woman to gain entrance to the party.
• Witnessing the sacred rituals of Bona Dea

These are serious charges and all involved will be called to account.

Further furtive coverage…
Pg 2 *'I only did it for a laugh' says Clodius, but who's laughing now?*
Pg 3—4 *Pretty Pompeia in on the plot?*
Pg 5 *'I sold him the dress, but he said it was for his mum,' tragic tailor's tale.*

Clodius was put on trial for disrupting a sacred festival. Cicero led the case for the prosecution. But JC refused to testify against a fellow Populares (even one that was clearly a troublemaker). Crassus paid off the jurors and Clodius was freed, vowing revenge against Cicero.

The scandal gave JC an opportunity to dump Pompeia. He'd spent all her money and she'd failed to give him a child. Besides, after the divorce JC could exploit his position as a single man and make yet another political match. Of course, in public JC's reasons for divorcing Pompeia were not quite so brutal. Instead Caesar implied that she'd known about Clodius' prank. He told people that:

My wife must be above suspicion.

49

Spain again

JC was soon on his way back to Spain. Now he was a propraetor he would be running the province as governor. However, his huge debt meant that his departure had to be delayed…

YOU DON'T KEEP UP THE PAYMENTS, YOU DON'T GET THE GOODS!

HOW AM I SUPPOSED TO GET TO SPAIN THEN?

WALK?

BAILIFF

Luckily Crassus bailed him out again.

JC was only in Spain for a year, but he certainly didn't hang around. When he arrived the Romans only controlled the southern part of the country. The northern half was controlled by bandits. For years they'd hidden in the hills and raided Roman villas and farms.

At first JC offered peace terms to the bandits, but they refused to come down from the mountains. So JC launched a campaign against them. He attacked towns suspected of supporting the outlaws. When some bandits fled to an island, JC tracked them down.

He didn't have enough of an army to fully occupy the country, but JC made sure Rome knew about his success in subduing the bandits (and grabbing their money).

FOR ROME LOVE FROM J.C

ROME 1,000 MILES

The trip to Spain had gone well for JC (and not just because of the loot). For the first time, he wore the scarlet cloak of a general. He found that he enjoyed commanding an army and got on very well with his troops.

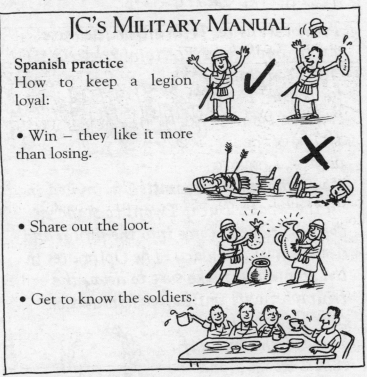

JC's MILITARY MANUAL

Spanish practice
How to keep a legion loyal:

• Win – they like it more than losing.

• Share out the loot.

• Get to know the soldiers.

JC had been so successful in Spain that the senate in Rome voted him a triumph.

Forum fact: Triumphs. After military victories Rome held huge parades in honour of the General. His soldiers would sing vulgar songs about him, and everyone would eat and drink to excess.

Of course, celebrating a triumph was exactly the sort of thing that JC would have loved to do but there was a problem...

JC's Secret Diary 61 BC

I've got a choice. I can either celebrate my triumph (and I certainly deserve it) OR I can stand for consul. I can't do both. If I have the parade, I have to stay outside the city until I'm invited in by the senate. But if I want to stand as consul I have to come into the forum and declare my candidacy. The Optimates in the senate will make sure to delay the triumph invite until after nominations close for consul.

I asked the senate if they'd let me stand for the consulship without turning up but they said, 'No dice.' So it's one or the other.

There's no contest really. There's only one game I'm interested in...

JC left his soldiers in Spain and rode back to Rome alone. He had the money, he had the fame, now all he needed was the power...

A THREE-HEADED MONSTER

In Roman elections fame and riches held the key to victory. By now Julius Caesar had plenty of both. The only real question was who the Optimates would try and get elected alongside him. They needed someone who'd stand up to JC. They needed someone to stop him from getting through his plans to help the poor. They needed someone about the same age as JC and just as exciting. Instead they chose someone else...

With Bibulus also elected for 59 BC, the Optimates probably breathed a sigh of relief. The whole point of having two consuls was that one could stop the other from changing things too much...

JC's Secret Diary 59 BC

I am finally a consul. My mother says she always knew I'd make it. If only my dad had been around to see it.

Anyway, the point is not just to get elected; it's to actually do something. If I'm to be as popular and famous as I should be, I'm going to need to do something really spectacular. I've been giving it some thought and I reckon I can become a hero amongst the poor people of Rome if I manage to give them more land to farm. At the moment rich people (like those windbags Cicero and Cato) run most of the public land. They use huge slave gangs to farm it and make massive amounts of money, but they take all the cash; none of it goes to the poor people of Rome.

The only problem is Bibulus. He's a puppet for his rich friends who run the land now. He's bound to block my plans. Still, I reckon I can handle Bibulus. And the rewards for succeeding are

> huge. If I do it I'll be the most popular consul since Uncle Marius, and he got elected consul seven times. It's definitely worth the risk...

JC needed a plan to sideline his fellow consul. So he decided to look around the forum for some support. He approached the two most powerful men in Rome. Pompey and Crassus were no longer in power but they still needed a friendly consul to protect their interests on the forum. JC offered them the chance to work together – unofficially, of course. Historians call this the 'First Triumvirate' (meaning the 'rule of three') but some Romans at the time were less impressed. They saw it as a threat to the officially elected magistrates. The writer Varro called it:

'THE THREE HEADED MONSTER'

Despite this opposition the Triumvirate was a superb partnership. Crassus supplied the money, Pompey had the troops and JC had the political office, as well as the personality to exploit it. Between them they could get people elected and, hopefully, pass new laws...

The first job the three men set themselves was passing JC's land bill. Pompey had a particular interest in this because he was still waiting to be given land on which he could settle the ex-soldiers from his many wars. Although it was traditional to give the soldiers land, Pompey's strained relations with the Optimates had left him (and his troops) out in the cold.

At first JC tried to get his bill through the senate. But the Optimates rallied around their leader in the senate, Cato. As the representatives of Rome's rich elite, they were furious that anyone would try and stop them exploiting public land. Cato was especially angry. He spoke against the bill for hours, and hours, and hours...

REPUBLICAN NEWS

59 BC

Senate stands shoulder to shoulder with Cato

There were outraged scenes in the senate last night as half of its membership asked to be put in jail. They were demanding their own arrest to show support for Cato. The Optimate leader had succeeded in talking for such a long time that the Julius Caesar was unable to hold a vote on his new land bill. The consul was so angry that he had Cato arrested.

As the guards took Cato away, dozens of senators declared they'd rather be in prison with Cato than in the senate with Caesar. This show of solidarity ensured Caesar's surrender; the bill has been withdrawn and Cato has been released.

Cato was unavailable for comment today and is said to be 'resting his voice'.

It was a rare political error, but JC wasn't the type of man to allow a little thing like the senate get in the way of his ambition. He tried a different tactic. His strength had always been his ability to woo the crowds of Rome, so now he took his bill direct to the people...

To appear as reasonable as possible JC first asked Bibulus if he had any objections. Encouraged by the senators' stand, the Optimate consul refused to even discuss the proposals with JC. So JC called a public meeting in the forum to vote on the bill. JC, Crassus and Pompey appeared on the platform...

JC had Pompey position his troops around the forum. When Bibulus and his supporters tried to vote against the bill the troops shouted them down and roughed them up. In the uproar Bibulus had a basket of dung tipped over his head. To make sure that no one in the senate got any nasty ideas, JC had the senators swear an oath, vowing not to overturn the new law.

Not surprisingly, Bibulus was pretty peeved (and smelly) after his run in at the forum. He called an emergency meeting of the senate. But even the most diehard Optimates knew that they'd lost to JC's superior political skill (and Bibulus' uselessness). Without the senate's backing Bibulus had to retreat to his house. There he declared that he would disrupt the political process by studying the skies for omens.

Forum fact: Omens. Romans were a superstitious bunch. There were several official augurs who'd check that the signs were right for official business to continue. If birds flew the wrong way or there was a storm it was thought the gods were angry. That was often enough to make Romans stop what they were doing.

JC didn't believe in omens and just ignored his fellow consul. He wasn't the only one. It became a popular joke around Rome to refer to the consulship, not of Caesar and Bibulus, but of 'Julius' and 'Caesar'.

But JC hadn't finished cementing his relationship with Pompey. He had another trick up the sleeve...

ALL HAIL MAGAZINE
WIFE SWAP SPECIAL 59 BC

Toga-ther at last! The happy couples.

A double marriage delight as Julia Caesar, daughter of the consul, Julius, marries Pompey the Great. And don't they make a 'Great' couple?

And consul Julius Caesar stakes his claim to Calpurnia, daughter of another of Rome's leading lights (and a friend of Pompey) Lucius Calpurnius Piso.

JC was planning for the future. His total disregard for Bibulus was illegal and could well land him in court. Certainly Cicero and Cato, who'd both lost land (as well as influence) during JC's consulship, would be planning to make life difficult for him as soon as he left office. So JC decided to strike first.

JC's Secret Diary 59 BC

I saw Clodius the other day. He's calmed down a bit since his cross-dressing escapades but he's still furious with Cicero. He's determined to become a tribune and prosecute him for killing the Catiline prisoners without a trial. I told him I'd do anything to help. It would serve that self-serving Cicero right to be up on a murder charge.
With a bit of encouragement from me I

think Clodius should be able to stop Cicero troubling me when I'm no longer consul. He won't be able to take me to court if he's already fighting off Clodius! As for Cato, getting him out of the way will need an altogether lighter touch. He's famous for being so incorruptible, principled and honourable. It's not like he's flamboyant and fun like me...

JC IV

Calpurnia

Clodius succeeded in becoming a tribune and successfully hounded Cicero into exile. Meanwhile, JC appointed Cato to govern the newly acquired island of Cyprus...

WE NEED SOMEONE WITH HONOUR AND INTEGRITY. OF COURSE, WE THOUGHT OF YOU.

YOU POMPOUS OLD GOAT.

WELL, IF YOU PUT IT LIKE THAT....

With his two enemies out of the way, JC could move on to the next stage of his incredible career...

THE FALL OF GAUL: PART I

JC's Secret Diary 58 BC

It's time for me to think of my own future. I could hang around in Rome and play politics some more. But to be honest I've been there, done that and got the toga. What I need is something exciting, something that will grab the imagination of future generations, something that will make me the greatest Roman of all time. What I really need is an army. I reckon I could become a general to rival Pompey himself. That's what I'm after, a game where there's some serious land (and fame) at stake...

Fortunately for JC Rome was also in need of a commander. For years restless barbarian tribes had been threatening Italy's northern border.

Romans like Julius Caesar saw their provinces as the very edge of civilization. Beyond their borders they believed that the world was populated by wild barbarians who didn't have roads, legions or even baths. Romans did trade with some of the tribes and even used some of the friendlier ones as allies but, in general, they were careful to make sure the barbarians stayed away from Roman civilization. The country of Gaul (modern-day France) lay just beyond JC's new provinces. It was full of wild tribes; each running their own areas...

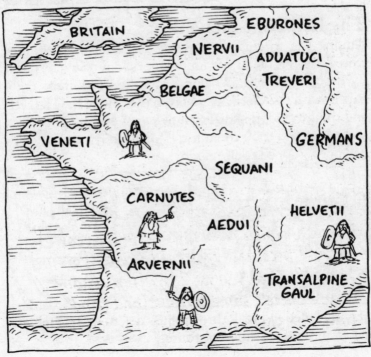

Now he was a proconsul, JC was appointed governor of Transalpine Gaul, Cisalpine Gaul and Illyricum for five years. There he would have command of a big army. Officially he would use these to defend Italy's northern borders. Unofficially he could use them to conquer new territory in Gaul.

Most of what we know about JC's tours of duty in Gaul we know from the man himself. JC's book was called *The Gallic War*.

THE BEST WAY TO GET YOUR NAME IN THE HISTORY BOOKS? WRITE 'EM YOURSELF!

The hell-bent Helvetii

Among the wilder tribes along Italy's northern border were the Helvetii, from modern-day Switzerland. JC described them as being 'embroiled in almost daily battles with the Germans'. Maybe that's why the Helvetii and their friends decided to move to Western Gaul.

Their route took them into Roman territory, but JC's defences stopped their march...

ROMAN LAND, NO ROAMIN' ALLOWED!

Having failed to break through JC's defences the Helvetii decided to take a different route.

JC's legions gave chase, catching up with them at the Helvetii town of Bibracte. Two thirds had already crossed the river there, but the Romans slaughtered the remaining third.

JC thought about trying to catch up to the rest of the Helvetii, but he was running low on supplies. His allies, the Aedui, weren't being very helpful, so instead he set out for the Aeduan capital to pick up some stores. The Helvetii saw the change of direction and thought it was a retreat. Foolishly, they attacked.

JC's MILITARY MANUAL

How to humiliate the Helvetii

- Send up traditional javelin welcome.

3 LINES OF ROMANS

- Stand firm against full frontal assault.

1 LINE 2 LINES

- Move one line to the right to meet attack on the right flank.

EEK

- Use gladius to make Swiss cheese of enemy.

- Seize Helvetii camp and loot.

When the Romans took the Helvetii camp, the full scale of the tribe's losses became clear. 258,000 had been killed....

Graciously, JC allowed what was left of the tribe to return to their villages near Geneva.

Arrogant Ariovistus

According to himself, JC was now a hero in Gaul.

JC's Secret Diary 58 BC

The rest of Gaul knows I mean business now. Most of the tribes sent delegates to congratulate me on a job well done.
Afterwards, they asked to see me in private to discuss another little 'German problem'.
Apparently the Sequani, a troublemaking tribe in the east, have been inviting German tribes into Gaul to join them in plundering the neighbours. The German leader, a bloke called Ariovistus,

is demanding more land. He keeps bringing more Germans across into Gaul. If he grabs more land he'll make the local tribes landless, and they'll march west seeking land for themselves. When they try and seize new lands all of the rest of Gaul will be in uproar (and there's nothing worse than a roaring Gaul). I will not stand for any foreigners invading Gaul (unless they're Roman). Time to teach these Germans a little lesson...

JC had to act carefully here. Ariovistus had been officially recognized as a friend of Rome under JC's own consulship. He couldn't just start a war with Ariovistus so JC decided to send letters instead...

Dear Ariovistus,
Can we meet up and discuss some state business, please?

Legion loyalty

JC was quite happy with the way the negotiations had gone. He came over as reasonable whereas Ariovistus appeared arrogant and rude. And he was rubbing his hands with glee at the thought of fighting the Germans. But his legionaries were less excited. Some started grumbling and said they wouldn't fight... JC needed to ensure that his legions were loyal, so he decided to call on his best troops.

Funnily enough, this won JC the loyalty of all his legions…

An interesting meeting

JC led his men towards the enemy. Ariovistus was much less confident when face to face with JC and his legionaries. He asked for a private meeting. Since this is what JC had said he'd wanted all along he could hardly refuse…

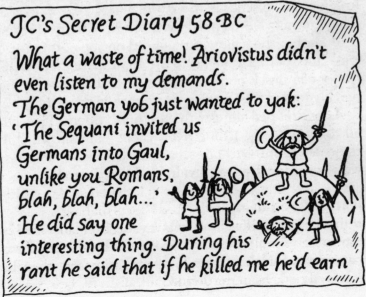

JC's Secret Diary 58 BC

What a waste of time! Ariovistus didn't even listen to my demands.
The German yob just wanted to yak:
'The Sequani invited us Germans into Gaul, unlike you Romans, blah, blah, blah…'
He did say one interesting thing. During his rant he said that if he killed me he'd earn

the gratitude of 'aristocrats and leaders at Rome'. He said they'd sent him messages. Clearly my enemies in Rome are waiting for me to make a mess of Gaul. Then there was more guff about how powerful his troops were. Boring! In the end I just left. Frankly it wouldn't surprise me if Ariovistus was still making his speech, with no one listening...

The Romans won the battle which followed in spectacular fashion. The two sides closed so quickly that the legionaries were unable to send up the traditional javelin welcome. The Germans advanced with their shields locked together but the legionaries jumped on top of the shield wall and pulled it apart with their bare hands. JC stationed himself on the far right of the Roman line and quickly routed the German warriors in front of him.

Ariovistus fled along with most of his troops. They ran all the way to the Rhine river where many drowned in their desperation to cross back to Germany. The rest were caught by Roman cavalry and slaughtered.

The bored Belgae

It had been a good year's campaigning. So JC decided to return to Cisalpine Gaul and spend the winter doing paperwork. But the winter had hardly finished when JC received news from northern Gaul...

JC's Secret Diary 57 BC

It seems the Belgae of northern Gaul are arming for war. They think with the Germans out of the picture we Romans will conquer the rest of Gaul. Well, you can't blame them, I suppose. Mind you, now they're actually preparing for war we should do the decent thing and give them one.

To be honest I'd much rather be out in the field with my legions than sat here dealing with all this governing nonsense. As soon as I can, I'll go 'pacify' the Belgae. It'll serve 'em right for trying it on with the best Roman general ever (that's me)...

JC raised two new legions and set out for what is now Belgium. Amazingly it only took him two weeks to reach the border...

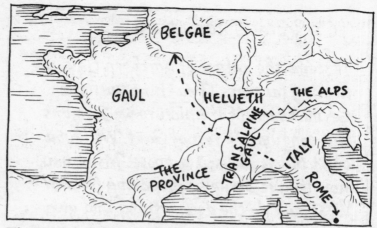

The Belgae had around 300,000 warriors from three tribes. At night the watch fires extended for seven miles around their camp.

With only 40,000 legionaries JC decided not to risk a full-frontal attack.

Amazingly, after a few small clashes the Belgae actually got bored of waiting and split up. JC quickly attacked two of the tribes, forcing their leaders to flee across the Channel. That just left the main troublemakers: the Nervii...

The Nervii's nasty surprise

JC now made a tactical error. Although he knew that the Nervii were nearby he ordered his men to camp. Usually some of the legionaries would build the camp while others stood watch, but this time JC decided to use far fewer men as a guard. The Nervii saw their chance...

JC describes the moment he realized they were under attack. He...

...had to see to everything at once. The flag must be unfurled, the trumpet sounded; the soldiers must be recalled from working on the defences, and all those gone some way off in search of material ... had to be ordered back to camp. He must draw up his battle line, encourage the men, give the signal. There was too little time, the enemy pressed on so fast, to complete these arrangements.

Luckily for JC, his officers rallied the men and the battle began.

On JC's left wing the tribal warriors found themselves against JC's best soldiers (including his favourite Xth legion). The Romans stopped the enemy's advance and began to push the Belgae back into the woods, with the Xth legion in pursuit.

But it was a different story on the Roman right. There the XIIth and VIIth legions were in trouble; in fact a few legionaries were already running away.

Immediately JC saw what the problem was. The Roman soldiers had huddled together so tightly that they had no room to use their swords. JC grabbed a shield from a fleeing legionary and plunged into the battle. Calling to his centurions by name, JC made his men open their ranks so they could use their weapons properly. Then he got his men to hold their line while at the same time moving around to face a new enemy attack on their flank. Even then the VIIth and XIIth legions faced defeat. Fortunately the commander of the Xth legion (a man called Labienus) saw the danger. He halted the pursuit of the enemy and came back to help.

Suddenly the Nervii were being attacked from behind. They fought bravely, standing on the bodies of their fallen comrades to launch missiles at the Romans, but soon they were almost wiped out.

JC the Not-So-Merciful

The Aduatuci had been on their way to help the Nervii when they heard what had happened to their allies. They returned to their fortified town and laughed at the Romans. They laughed even harder at the siege towers that JC had built to take the town.

When the Gauls saw the Roman siege tower moving they stopped laughing. The next morning the Romans broke down the gates and the siege was over.

JC may have slaughtered thousands of Gauls, but so far he'd allowed any survivors to return home, as long as they promised to behave. But this time he was not-so-Mr Nice Guy. He sold the whole town (including the inhabitants) to Roman traders, then he sent (most) of the proceeds back to Rome…

75

A VISIT WITH FRIENDS

While he'd been careering through Gaul, JC had ignored his own career in Rome. Although he still had a few years left as Governor he was already looking to get an extension. But, while he'd been away, there'd been some changes (and some trouble) in Rome...

JC's Secret Diary 57 BC
Clodius might be my man in Rome, but apparently he's been being a bit mischievous (typical). He's been giving free corn to the people. Personally I thought it was a nice touch; keeping the citizens fed, but apparently Pompey is fed up. (Clodius has been stealing his glory.) With me out of the picture the Optimates have brought Cicero and Cato back.

It's only a matter of time before they start kicking up a stink about recalling me to Rome. They'll haul me into court for breaking the rules when I was consul. And they'll definitely try to stop me from standing as consul again. They're such an ungrateful bunch of so-and-sos. I mean, they keep asking the question, 'What has JC ever done for us?' Oh, I don't know, just secured our borders with Gaul, filled the treasury with gold, the markets with slaves and brought glory to the city of Rome...

They won't succeed. If there's one thing I'm good at; it's the game of politics...

Over the winter of 57–56 BC the rumour mill in Rome was working overtime. Everyone knew that JC, Pompey and Crassus had been holding discussions, getting ready for some big announcement. JC's enemies hoped that Pompey would split from JC. That would leave the Governor of Cisalpine Gaul an easy target for their lawyers (or assassins). But JC was far too clever to let that happen.

In the spring of 56 BC, Rome's politicians decamped to Lucca, a town just inside JC's province of Cisalpine Gaul...

REPUBLICAN NEWS

59 BC

Threesome seal deal at Lucca

Five Year Plan suits JC, Pompey and Crassus
The political deal of the decade was sealed here today as Rome's top three men met among the hills of northern Italy. Hundreds of Rome's senators accepted Julius Caesar's invitation to witness the historic meeting between Crassus, Pompey and himself. Officially, of course, any deal is just a private agreement between friends, but unofficially everyone knows that these three men will run Rome for as long as the deal holds.

While the three main men were locked in intense discussions Rome's great and good enjoyed the fine wines, beautiful countryside and top-notch bathing facilities of Lucca.

THIS DEAL SHOULD GET THEM OUT OF ANY HOT WATER.

Finally an announcement was made that once again the triumvirate would carve up power between them. But this time there are a few modifications:

• Crassus and Pompey are to be consuls for the next year.
• JC's command in Gaul is to be extended by a further five years.

- Crassus is to take command of an equal army and head for Syria (to stop the pesky Parthians).
- Pompey is to command the army in Spain. He'll also take control of corn distribution in Rome.

Sources close to the discussion say the main sticking point was JC's continued support for Clodius in Rome. Pompey told this paper, 'JC really skirted around the issue of that cross-dressing fop, Clodius. But we've got a promise that JC will give him a good dressing down.'

JC had the extension of his command that he wanted, while Pompey and Crassus were satisfied with their new roles. With the deal done, the meeting broke up.

It was the last time JC would see either Pompey or Crassus alive.

THE FALL OF GAUL: PART II

Before JC had travelled to Lucca he'd been confident that 'the whole of Gaul was pacified'. In fact, he was so confident he was even planning a quick invasion of Britain. But now there was trouble brewing once more. The problem this time was the people who lived along Gaul's northern coast. They were expert sailors and their towns were well defended by the sea.

During the winter one tribe, the Veneti, took some Romans prisoner.

JC began to plan his revenge. He ordered one of his commanders (a man called Decimus Brutus) to build dozens of Roman ships on a river in the south of Gaul. In the spring, the ships were sailed up the coast and into battle.

A LARGE PORTION OF SHIPS, PLEASE.

But if JC thought a Roman fleet would even up the odds he was wrong…

ROMAN SHIP

POWERED BY OARS SO BLOWN OFF COURSE BY STRONG WINDS

DEEP KEELS SNAG ON UNDERWATER ROCKS AND REEFS

ROMAN BATTERING RAM USELESS AGAINST VENETI OAK

LEATHER SAILS DON'T BREAK IN HIGH WINDS

STICK TO THE ROADS, ROMANS!

VENETI SHIP

BUILT SOLIDLY OF OAK

SHALLOW KEELS AVOID REEFS AND ROCKS

HIGH SIDES PROTECT AGAINST WAVES AND ROMAN GRAPPLING HOOKS

The Veneti ships were just too strong for the Romans. But JC refused to be beaten. He soon worked out a way to scupper the Veneti.

JC's Military Manual

How to take the wind out of Veneti sails
• Attach sharpened hooks to long poles
• Use hooks to cut ropes attaching the sails to Veneti ships
• Laugh at Veneti as their ships drift in the seas without wind power
• Use oarsome Roman ships to take on Veneti one by one.

Without ships, the Veneti were at JC's mercy; or lack of it. He had their leaders slaughtered and sold the rest of the population into slavery.

A bridge too far?

JC decided to put off an invasion of Britain for another year. But as 56 BC became 55 BC he was faced with yet another problem...

JC's Secret Diary 55 BC
Oh, for Jupiter's sake! Can't a man just invade an island when he wants to? I'm almost ready for the invasion of Britain but some gang of Germans has apparently just crossed the Rhine into Gaul.

They sent a message asking if they can move in, but I've told them already: 'You can't stay here!' I will NOT have foreigners invading Gaul. That's my job.

JC marched for the Rhine. He smashed the German camp. Then the Roman cavalry chased the survivors (including women and children) back across the Rhine, killing more on the way.

JC could have left it at that, but he wanted to teach the Germans a lesson...

JC's MILITARY MANUAL

How to build a disposable bridge
I: Build bridge in ten days flat.

SHAME IT DOESN'T COME FLAT PACKED.

II: Visit locals.

BYE!

III: Return to Gaul, burning the bridge after you leave. *Make sure you do this in the right order!*

This time JC appeared to have gone too far, even for some of his countrymen. Back in Rome questions were being raised in the senate (no surprise by whom)...

REPUBLICAN NEWS

55 BC

JC the war criminal?

Cato Charges Caesar
Last night Optimate leader Cato condemned Julius Caesar's harsh conduct of the war in Gaul. He told senators that JC should be 'handed over to the German tribes as a war criminal'. When it was pointed out that JC's campaign had resulted in huge amounts of gold and slaves arriving in Rome, Cato replied, 'How can we spread civilization if we act like barbarians?'

Cato stands alone on this issue. With the mob outside clamouring for more celebratory feasts, the senators ignored him. Instead they voted to award JC more accolades and days of triumph.

Try as they might, JC's enemies in Rome couldn't dent his popularity...

{ JC'S BRITISH HOLIDAY }

By now JC was getting quite cocky. Despite the approach of winter he decided pull off another famous feat…

JC's Secret Diary 54 BC

Finally I'm off to Britain. People might ask why? Well here are my reasons:

I: They've been stirring up trouble among the Gauls

II: I hear they've got some fine gold and pearls

III: I'll be the first Roman to visit the island

IV: The Roman people will love it (especially if point number II is true)

V: It'll really get on Cato's wick! It's a bit too late in the year to launch a full invasion so I'll travel light. I'll take two legions and some cavalry. Nothing fancy. Just enough for a quick visit...

Late in 54 BC, almost 100 ships set off from Gaul across the English channel. In the heavy seas the infantry ships were separated from the cavalry transports. Then, as the ships approached Dover, JC realized the cliff tops were swarming with fearsome British warriors. JC describes the British as dying their skin blue and shaving their whole bodies, except for their heads and the upper lips ... pretty fearsome.

The fleet sailed up the coast to Deal, in Kent. There they found beaches, but the deep-bottomed Roman boats couldn't get close enough. Perhaps JC should have taken the hint, but he was determined to land his men.

The legionaries were told to swim or wade ashore.

WELCOME TO BRITANNIA

But they faced chariot attacks, cavalry charges and missiles.

It looked pretty bleak for JC (typical British holiday, really). But then a legionary from the Xth grabbed the legion's eagle standard and charged forward. He yelled that he'd rather lose the eagle than his dignity. The punishment for soldiers who allowed their standard to be captured was death. With this in mind the Roman infantry made a final charge for land, driving off the British.

Despite the fact that his cavalry were yet to arrive, JC took some hostages and congratulated himself on reaching Britain.

87

It never rains but it pours

Just when JC thought he was over the worst, disaster struck again. A violent storm drove the cavalry transports even further away from Britain. The weather was so bad some ships retreated all the way back to Gaul. The infantry ships had not been properly dragged up the beach because their big keels made it too much hard work. Instead they had been left at anchor off the coast. Several ships were wrecked and most of the others were damaged.

The storm showed the British just how weak the Romans actually were.

Taking advantage, the tribes attacked one legion while it was out foraging for food a short way from the camp. Fortunately, the Xth saw what was happening and rushed to the rescue, again driving the British away. By now, however, JC had seen enough of Britain (for a while anyway).

If there was one thing that JC was absolutely expert at, it was writing reports which showed how great he was. Despite the near disaster in Britain, Rome voted for another 20-day triumphal celebration for JC, who had heroically claimed Britain for the Romans. For JC, this was proof that Britain was worth another visit…

British pluck vs Roman luck

JC spent the winter assembling a huge fleet (in fact the Channel didn't see a bigger fleet until 1944). This time almost 700 ships set out to invade Britain.

The Romans landed in Britain unopposed. JC thought the Brits were frightened by the sheer number of ships, but the tribes had holed up in a fort just a few miles inland. Quickly the Romans stormed the stronghold and pursued the tribal warriors. But, once again, JC's ships were not properly beached.

A storm damaged every ship in the fleet and sank 40 of them. JC had to recall his troops and send to Gaul for carpenters to repair the damage. Once they were repaired, he finally brought the ships on to the beach. This time, to make sure, JC had protective trenches built around them.

Meanwhile, the British tribes had elected a man called Cassivellaunus to command their warriors. He'd seen enough of the legions to know that taking them on in open battle was foolhardy. So instead he used a different tactic...

IT'S A DRIVE-BY ATTACK! FEELS MORE LIKE A DRIVE-THROUGH!

JC ignored these small chariot raids. He kept his men marching north, in search of a place where the British would be forced to fight. He found what he was looking for when he reached the river Thames near what is now Brentford. Along the north bank the British tribes were ready for battle.

Despite being in a weak position – far from home, with a river to cross and a bunch of bloodthirsty warriors facing them – the Romans did what they did best. They crossed the river, seized the north bank and put the British to flight. But JC didn't have time to taste victory. News arrived from the fleet–it was under attack.

JC then had two pieces of good luck. First the men guarding the ships managed to hold off the British barbarians. Then, several local tribes turned traitor. Cassivellaunus was now isolated and eventually surrendered.

This was good luck indeed because by now JC was thinking of leaving...

JC's Secret Diary 54 BC
I've fought enough battles to know when luck isn't on my side.
Anyway, the Brits are just a bunch of barbarians (they even drive their chariots on the wrong side of the road). Now they've

been beaten at least they know the power of Rome...

I'll tell the senate that I've brought the Roman army to the edge of the known world (which is true), that I've taken lots of hostages (which is less true) and that I'm sure there's plenty of treasure to be found there (which is not true at all). The weather's terrible, the food's awful and the locals are revolting. Frankly I'm sick of the sight of Britain, and I'm sure they're sick of the sight of me.

Still, I've won glory for Rome and myself. Just wait until the people hear of my adventures...they'll love it!)

Quickly JC packed his troops into the transports and set out for Gaul. It was the last Britain would see of the Romans for almost 100 years...

GOOD RIDDANCE, I SAY!

91

THE FALL OF GAUL: PART III

The terrible weather in Britain wasn't the only reason JC hurried back to Gaul. Yet again there was trouble brewing...

REPUBLICAN NEWS

54 BC

Romans massacred!
Galling Gaul plays vile trick

Rome has suffered its worst defeat in Gaul since the arrival of Julius Caesar.

With the Roman proconsul taking a British break, a Gaul by the name of Ambiorix is leading a new rebellion against our forces.

Realizing that there was no way that the Gauls could beat us in a fair fight, awful Ambiorix has resorted to low cunning. He pretended to be a friend of Rome and targeted two new commanders.

Sabinus and Cotta were told that they faced an attack by rogue Germans. Ambiorix persuaded them to leave camp and join up with their comrades some 60 miles away.

Foolishly the two men decided to follow the slippery Gaul's advice and hastily packed up camp. But, soon after they left, they were ambushed by Gauls. Trapped in a ravine, the Roman soldiers were slaughtered, only a few survived to tell the tale. Sabinus and Cotta were lost in battle.

The whole of Northern Gaul is in chaos once more.

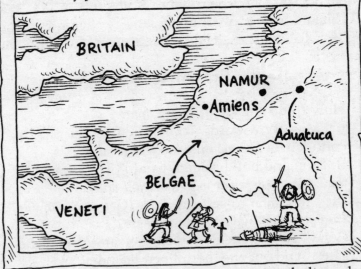

Ambiorix commanded a large army, including the remains of the Nervii and the Aduatuci. These tribes had learnt a thing or two from fighting against the Romans over the last few years. Now, when they laid siege to another Roman camp, they used Roman tactics, including siege towers.

The camp commander was able to get a message through to JC at Amien. It probably went something like this:

Can't hold out much longer... Gauls every where... Men fighting bravely but fire in camp... Hurry up!

JC had only two legions with him. That meant he had around 7,000 men, compared to Ambiorix's 60,000. But JC knew a trick or two himself...

JC's MILITARY MANUAL

How to do the small camp scam

I: March towards the enemy, appearing confident. (*The men need to feel positive.*)

II: Stop and build a small camp. (*The enemy will think you have fewer men than you do.*)

III: Order men to act panicked. (*Get them running around yelling 'We're all going to die!!'*)

IV: When the enemy attack the camp, open the gates, send out the disciplined legions.

V: Enjoy victory.

The ruse worked. The Gauls were driven off. When JC reached the camp he found that nine out of ten Roman soldiers were injured. It had been a very close-run thing.

A Gallic winter

JC knew that he had to improve the odds before the winter was finished and the Gauls revolted again. He sent one of his officers to Cisalpine Gaul to raise two new legions, and then sat down and wrote a letter...

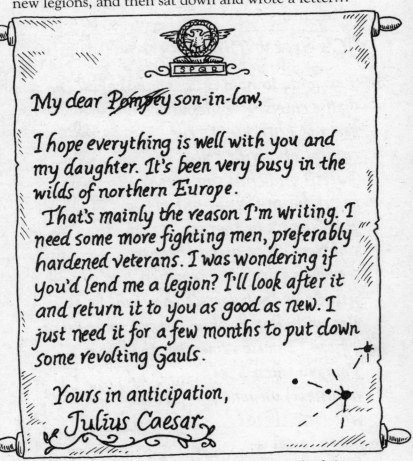

My dear ~~Pompey~~ son-in-law,

I hope everything is well with you and my daughter. It's been very busy in the wilds of northern Europe.

That's mainly the reason I'm writing. I need some more fighting men, preferably hardened veterans. I was wondering if you'd lend me a legion? I'll look after it and return it to you as good as new. I just need it for a few months to put down some revolting Gauls.

Yours in anticipation,
Julius Caesar

Within months three extra legions had reached Amiens. JC didn't even wait for the end of winter. Instead he marched out immediately and headed for the land of the Nervii. The tribe's cattle were slaughtered and any people nearby were sold into slavery. Crops were destroyed and once again the Nervii were forced to give hostages.

But JC knew that the rebellion wasn't going to die out just like that...

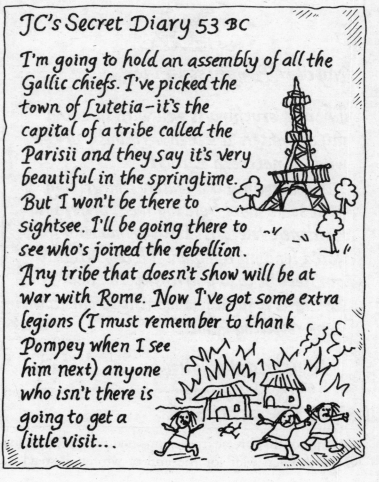

JC's Secret Diary 53 BC

I'm going to hold an assembly of all the Gallic chiefs. I've picked the town of Lutetia – it's the capital of a tribe called the Parisii and they say it's very beautiful in the springtime. But I won't be there to sightsee. I'll be going there to see who's joined the rebellion. Any tribe that doesn't show will be at war with Rome. Now I've got some extra legions (I must remember to thank Pompey when I see him next) anyone who isn't there is going to get a little visit...

Sure enough, at the meeting in Lutetia (modern-day Paris, in case you hadn't guessed) there were several notable absences. Within weeks JC had visited the truants.

He captured Acco, chief of the Senones, cracked the Carnutes, mopped up the Menapii and trounced the Treveri. Which only left Ambiorix and the Eburones. Maybe JC and his legions were a bit tired after all that marching. Perhaps that explains why he asked other tribes to join in against his next opponents...

The Governor of Gaul, Julius Caesar, invites everyone to a Pillage and Plunder party.

Come and help sack the cities, kill the crops and capture the cattle of the rogue Gauls.

A special game of Ambush Ambiorix has been arranged.

(Bring your own battle)

JC never managed to capture Ambiorix, but the Eburones were destroyed.

JC called another meeting of the Gallic chieftains and had Acco beaten to death in front of them.

As JC travelled back to northern Italy for the winter of 53–52 BC he hoped that he'd tamed Gaul's rebellious tribes, but he was badly mistaken...

Valiant Vercingetorix

Over the winter, various tribes met to discuss their tactics. They elected a chief from the Arverni tribe to lead them in their desperate struggle against Rome – Vercingetorix.

The chiefs agreed a signal to spark the new uprising: Roman traders in the Loire valley suddenly found themselves on the wrong end of a massacre...

Vercingetorix knew that JC was stuck in his province of Transalpine Gaul. So the Gallic general split his army. Vercingetorix himself led a force towards the Bituriges, who had yet to join the rebellion. The rest, under the command of Lucterius, marched on the border of JC's province, hoping to cut the Roman governor off from his troops stationed in the north...

A tale of three sieges

JC wasn't the type to sit around and wait for the Gauls to attack. Instead, he raised what soldiers he could find and, ignoring the snow-covered roads, rode out to war as fast as he could.

The speed with which JC covered the ground in Gaul took everyone by surprise. He was able to stop Lucterius' advance and forced Vercingetorix to head south by threatening Arveni lands. Finally he was able to link up with the majority of his men in the north.

Vercingetorix's first move had failed. He had to change tactics. The tribes were told to burn the land, leaving nothing for JC and his army to eat. The Bituriges appeared to be quite happy with the plan but wanted to defend their capital, Avaricum.

IT'S SO WELL DEFENDED, JC WILL NEVER TAKE IT.

Within days the siege of Avaricum had begun.

JC's forces surrounded the town while Vercingetorix camped a few miles away. The Gaul planned to harass the Romans while they concentrated on seizing the town.

JC's Secret Diary 52 BC

The Gauls have learnt a lot about siege warfare recently. They've been lassoing our grappling hooks, setting fire to our siege ramps and building up the city walls to make it harder to attack. We're under constant fire from Gallic archers above. Whenever we kill a Gaul another takes his place.

> To make matters worse, we're running really low on supplies. Vercingetorix is camped nearby and attacks anyone we send out for food. My allies, the Boii and the Aedui, keep saying they'll bring food but there's always some delay (I reckon they're thinking about changing sides). I can't let the legions die from starvation. Maybe it's time to actually end the siege...

JC offered his soldiers the chance to withdraw from Avaricum but they refused. But JC wasn't the only one having difficulty. Vercingetorix was also running low on supplies. He'd tried sending a garrison out of Avaricum to attack the Romans, but had failed. So he began to plan a retreat.

Vercingetorix had reckoned on retreating without the town's citizens. When they heard that their army was planning to abandon them they raised such a stink that the Romans knew all about Vercingetorix's plan. The very next day the Romans attacked. It was raining heavily, but this time the legionaries broke through the city walls. 40,000 Gallic men, women and children were killed. Vercingetorix retreated, but told his followers not to lose heart.

EASY FOR HIM TO SAY!

He blamed the Bituriges for the defeat; they'd wanted to defend Avaricum and had promised that the town was secure. They'd been wrong.

Gergovia

JC raided the stores in Avaricum before setting off for Gergovia, the capital city of Vercingetorix's own tribe, the Arverni. The race was on. Vercingetorix moved his army down the western bank of the Allier river, burning bridges as he went. Meanwhile, JC marched along the Eastern bank. Vercingetorix arrived at Gergovia five days before JC and set about defending the town.

Now JC faced a critical problem. The revolt had now spread to JC's Gallic allies...

JC's Secret Diary 52BC
This uprising is more serious than I thought. I was expecting 10,000 Aeduan troops to join me, but it turns out they were heading for Vercingetorix instead. Apparently their chief told them that I'd massacred my Aeduan commanders. The soldiers were pretty put out by this lie and killed a bunch of Romans that were travelling with them. I had to ride out to meet the column to convince them that I hadn't killed their

friends. Luckily two Aeduan commanders came with me. By rights I could kill them all for murdering Romans. But I think it would be better to forget this little episode. If I show them some mercy maybe they'll fall into line again.

Still, if even the Aedui are mulling over mutiny, the odds are stacking up against us...

JC couldn't trust any of the Gauls now. He needed to break off the siege of Gergovia and rally all his forces in one spot (away from the big Gallic armies).

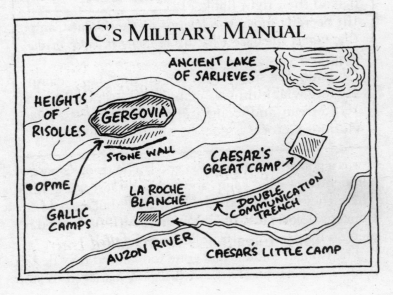

JC's MILITARY MANUAL

ANCIENT LAKE OF SARLIEVES →

HEIGHTS OF RISOLLES

GERGOVIA

STONE WALL

CAESAR'S GREAT CAMP

●OPME

LA ROCHE BLANCHE

GALLIC CAMPS

DOUBLE COMMUNICATION TRENCH

AUZON RIVER

CAESAR'S LITTLE CAMP

JC stationed two legions on La Roche Blanc. They were connected to his main camp by two trenches, each 12 feet wide. What he needed was a show of force at Gergovia that would cover his retreat...

JC's Military Manual

How to retreat at Gergovia:

I: Pretend to move cavalry to Opme. (*Dress up the baggage mules like cavalry by giving riders spare armour and sticks to look like javelins.*)

II: Wait for the Gauls to move their men to defend their right flank.

III: Secretly move the legions to the Great Camp (*the Gauls can't see what we're doing because of the trenches.*)

IV: Launch a surprise attack on the Gallic camp at Gergovia, killing as many Gauls as possible.

V: Retreat and congratulate the troops on a glorious victory.

It was a good plan; maybe too good. The troops smashed through the Gallic camp and reached Gergovia's walls. There they were supposed to fall back, but instead the Roman soldiers pressed on. Vercingetorix marshalled his men on the Heights of Risolles and charged.

The Roman soldiers had gone too far and now fled in confusion. Fortunately the Xth legion managed to stop

Vercingetorix's advance. But not before the Romans had lost 46 centurions and 700 soldiers at Gergovia.

When JC rallied his men the next day he congratulated them on their bravery, but he gave them a good ticking off for not following orders…

NEXT TIME YOU HEAR THE ORDER TO RETREAT WHAT ARE YOU GOING TO DO?

RETREAT!

JC would need all the bravery his troops could muster. The Roman position was dire. Behind them the Arverni were elated at their victory at Gergovia, on the flank the Bituriges were fighting mad at the destruction of their cities, and in front of them the Aedui had finally gone over to Vercingetorix.

A lesser leader than Julius Caesar would have taken the hint and retreated to the safety of his Roman province. But JC refused.

Alesia

Instead, JC marched his men north, pillaging Aeduan territory as they went. Outside Lutetia he met up with several legions that had been waiting there. Within a few weeks JC was ready for another fight.

To the south, Vercingetorix ordered part of his army to begin attacking the borders of the Roman province. The rest he took to the city of Alesia. From there he could harass JC if the Romans marched south towards the trouble. This is exactly what happened, and the two sides met somewhere near Dijon. Despite Vercingetorix's superiority in cavalry, his attack failed.

In fact Vercingetorix was forced to withdraw into Alesia itself.

It soon became clear that the Gauls were facing another difficult siege. It would require a huge effort on the Romans' part but Alesia gave JC a great opportunity to end the revolt. So he began to prepare for a third siege...

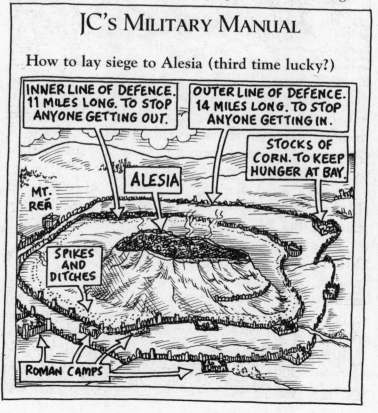

JC's MILITARY MANUAL

How to lay siege to Alesia (third time lucky?)

INNER LINE OF DEFENCE. 11 MILES LONG. TO STOP ANYONE GETTING OUT.

OUTER LINE OF DEFENCE. 14 MILES LONG. TO STOP ANYONE GETTING IN.

STOCKS OF CORN. TO KEEP HUNGER AT BAY.

ALESIA

MT. REA

SPIKES AND DITCHES

ROMAN CAMPS

JC's army numbered around 70,000. But he knew that somewhere in Gaul 250,000 warriors were preparing to come to Alesia's aid. All the Roman could do was wait... The siege dragged on and things inside Alesia soon became desperate. There was no food for the local population. Vercingetorix considered his options:

I: Surrender.

II: Try and break out.

III: Eat the old people.

107

Instead, Vercingetorix tried to evacuate the townspeople. Thousands of women, children and old men were kicked out of the town. They approached JC and asked if he'd take them in as slaves. But JC refused; he left the people to starve where they were. Why did he do this? Well, he had problems of his own. The 250,000 Gallic warriors had just arrived...

Alas, Alesia

JC's legions manned their posts all the way around Alesia. After two attacks by the new Gallic army the Romans were still in position, but everyone knew the next attack would be decisive. Not surprisingly the Gauls planned the raid very carefully.

I: First the Gauls sent a strong force to the one place on the line where the Romans hadn't finished their wall.

II: Next they attacked the two Roman camps in the south.

JC himself was forced to lead the defence, ordering his men to put aside their javelins and engage with their swords. His scarlet cloak was seen by the legionaries and they pushed forward.

Then came the moment of triumph...

JC had sent some cavalry outside the Roman defences. Suddenly the Gauls were being attacked from behind. They panicked and JC was able to finish them off.

> ## JC's Secret Diary 52 BC
> I always knew coming to Gaul would be a gamble and it's paid off. All Gaul is under Roman control. (Well, let's hope so anyway.)
>
> I've arranged for the tribes to pay an annual tribute to Rome. But I've told them they can collect it themselves. I've →

also decided to be merciful to the Aedui and the Arverni. I've learnt that there's no point in angering a Gaul more than necessary.

The rest of the prisoners are being put to good use. Every man in the legions will get a bonus.

They really deserve it after all that fighting. Besides, who knows when I'll need the legions to be loyal to me again? Vercingetorix surrendered to me in front of my camp. He's a fine fellow and I think I'll hold him prisoner for a while. I'll show him off to the people of Rome before I kill him. They'll be amazed to see me lead him out in chains along the forum during the triumph parade...

You might think that JC was right to expect a huge celebration when he returned to Rome. In the past seven years he'd brought all of Gaul under Roman control, he'd fought off German invaders and he'd brought the Romans to the edge of the known world. But while JC had been away, things in Rome had changed. And, for JC, they hadn't changed for the better...

THE DEATH OF A THREE-HEADED MONSTER

JC had always loved his daughter, Julia. Not only was she his only child, but her marriage to Pompey bound the former general to JC. Such political marriages were common in Rome and the end of such a marriage could severely damage an alliance. So, when JC heard of his daughter's death in 54 BC, he grieved but knew he would have to try and get Pompey to agree to a new alliance…

ALL HAIL MAGAZINE
WIFE SWAP SPECIAL! 54 BC

Following the death of his daughter, Julius Caesar has moved quickly to offer Pompey a substitute spouse.
'I've got this nice niece, Octavia. She's 12, just the right age for marrying off,' said JC, speaking from his headquarters in Gaul. 'We all miss Julia but Octavia is fit and healthy…'
As part of the deal. JC would divorce his current wife, Calpurnia (his third). He's offered

to marry Pompey's daughter, completing a fresh forum foursome.

There's no news yet from Pompey. Unusually for a top Roman it seems that Pompey actually loved his wife. It is said that the great man is actually mourning his dead wife and child.

Perhaps he's not ready for the marriage market.

Pompey turned down the offer. You might think that JC was being heartless. His daughter had only just died. But JC had read the political situation in Rome exactly right. Pompey was beginning to draw close to JC's mortal enemies: the Optimates. Two years after Julia's death Pompey *did* marry again. His new wife was a member of a leading Optimate family.

The three-headed monster loses a head

For a while after Pompey's marriage JC probably didn't worry too much; after all, he was far too busy fighting Gauls. Besides, if Pompey did let him down, there was always Crassus to back him up...

As part of their deal a few years before, Crassus had been given an army in Roman-controlled Syria. In 53 BC, he led this army into war against the Parthians. But Crassus was a much better banker than he was a general. The Romans were butchered. Crassus himself ended up heading to the Parthian king's court (his body wasn't allowed to come too). There his skull was used as a prop in a play...

ALAS, POOR CRASSUS, I KNEW HIM WELL.

CHORTLE!

Clodius vs Milo

Then things got even worse. While JC had been away Roman politics had been dominated by two gangs. Cross-dressing Clodius (who had been backed by Caesar in the past) and Titus Annius Milo (who was still backed by Pompey) fought for control of the streets and the people. In 52 BC the feud came to a bloody end...

Clodius was ambushed and killed by Milo's gladiators. News of the murder sparked riots in Rome. In honour of their fallen leader, Clodius' supporters held the funeral in the forum. Then some bright spark decided to put the funeral pyre in the senate house, completely destroying the building.

Pompey steps up

The violence that followed left Rome in turmoil. Elections couldn't take place because of marauding gangs. The senate needed someone to restore order. They needed someone with an army, someone ruthless that they could order around. Pompey was just the man for the job.

REPUBLICAN NEWS

52 BC

Pompey appointed sole consul

In a break with Roman tradition the traditionalists in the senate have invited Pompey to be sole consul for the next year. Perhaps it's surprising that the great man wasn't appointed dictator, but as a close friend of Cato said, 'We trust Pompey to stop the violence in Rome, but we don't trust him that much.'

Within hours of the announcement Pompey moved his troops into Rome and occupied the forum. Titus Annius Milo was arrested and charged with the murder of Clodius.

'I might not be dictator but that won't stop me from dictating what happens,' said Pompey. To prove the point Pompey's legionaries have spread out across the city. It's apparent that gang warfare is no match for soldiers trained for real warfare.

By 51 BC the crisis had passed. Pompey had restored order. Milo was found guilty and sent into exile. But Pompey's new found friendship with the Optimates was a setback for JC...

JC's Secret Diary 51 BC

Those overconfident Optimates in Rome are demanding I give up my command in Gaul. They reckon the war is over (which is true). But it's obvious they only want me back in the city to put me on trial. They reckon I broke the law when I was consul. Well I'm not going to stand for it. Instead, I'll wait until I can stand as consul again. Then they won't dare touch me!

It's not like I don't have stuff to do here. I'm writing up my notes on the war. It's a rip-roaring tale of historic heroic deeds done by a skilled and merciful commander by the name of

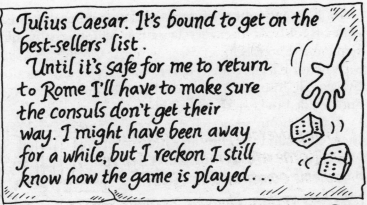

Julius Caesar. It's bound to get on the best-sellers' list.

Until it's safe for me to return to Rome I'll have to make sure the consuls don't get their way. I might have been away for a while, but I reckon I still know how the game is played...

JC had some solid support in Rome. The tribunes Gaius Scribonus Curio and Mark Antony rejected any proposals to bring him back. Whenever anyone suggested that JC give up his command, they replied that Pompey should give up his as well. The result was stalemate. JC continued to write his book and moved, along with one legion, to Cisalpine Gaul.

Suddenly JC was further weakened. The death of Crassus had left Syria exposed to Parthian attacks. More soldiers were needed. Pompey said he'd send one legion, as long as JC did the same. JC had to agree. But when Pompey came to choose his legion he chose the one he'd lent to JC in 53 BC. So instead of losing one legion, JC lost two.

WHAT A CHEAP TRICK!

As JC waved them off to Rome, he paid each man a sum of gold. At the very least the legionaries would remember him fondly.

When the legions arrived in Rome they weren't sent to Syria at all. Instead, Pompey declared the emergency over and decided to keep them in Italy.

Again Antony suggested that Pompey and JC lay down their commands at the same time. But the Optimates weren't prepared to give up power that easily. Finally they made their move...

REPUBLICAN NEWS

49 BC

Consuls call on Pompey to defend the state

There were astonishing scenes at the forum today as Pompey was finally appointed dictator. He is charged with defending the state against the rogue general, Julius Caesar.

The tribunes, including Mark Antony, attempted to block the decree, but in uproar the senators attacked them, forcing them from the forum. They were last seen heading north to join JC.

JC declared public enemy
Julius Caesar has several legions just a few weeks march away from Italy, while Pompey's legions are all the way over in Spain. But the dashing dictator is confident he can win any fight. 'I'm not scared,' Pompey told this newspaper last night, 'I have only to stamp my feet and legions will rise up to follow me.'

Pompey's supporters will be hoping that that's true, and that he doesn't stub his toe.

War was now inevitable.

CIVIL WAR

JC's headquarters at Ravenna was a few miles north of the river Rubicon. In Roman times, the river divided the province of Cisalpine Gaul from the rest of Italy. In early January 49 BC, Mark Antony and his fellow tribune arrived at Ravenna.

JC didn't let them recover from their tiring journey. Instead he called his troops into formation. He needed to make sure that his soldiers would stay loyal to him in the coming months. He showed them the exhausted tribunes to prove to that the senate had broken ancient Roman laws protecting the tribunes of the people.

Most were convinced and remained loyal to their commander. But Labienus, who'd served with JC through the years in Gaul, returned to Rome. JC must have been upset by this betrayal. He packed up all of Labienus' belongings and sent them off after his former friend.

The Rubicon

JC was never one for the cautious approach in war. On the night of the 10 January 49 BC, his one legion stood at the banks of the river Rubicon. There was a pause. Everyone knew that crossing the river meant fighting their fellow Romans. But JC was ready for such a gamble. As a child JC had played dice (a popular pastime for Roman kids), perhaps that's why he's reported to have used these words as he ordered his army across the river...

The die is cast

With these famous words, JC crossed the Rubicon and invaded his homeland.

Pompey's retreat
JC's advance was remarkable.

Within weeks JC had taken the towns of eastern Italy. In fact, most of the local garrisons ended up joining him. At Corfinium three legions held the town. After a brief siege they surrendered. Several senior politicians were handed over to JC.

The road to Rome was now open and Pompey was in a terrible situation. His best soldiers were in Spain. The legions he'd been confident of raising in Italy hadn't appeared. The troops that he did have were far from loyal; several had already gone over to JC. In the city itself JC's supporters were growing in confidence. It was time for Pompey to leave.

A fleet was prepared at Brundisium to take Pompey across to Greece. There he hoped to find fresh troops and, more importantly, money to fund his campaign.

Most of his supporters in the senate decided to take the trip as well. After all, they all remembered what had happened when Marius had occupied the city and they feared that JC would do the same.

Instead of occupying Rome, JC pursued Pompey. Repeatedly he sent messages asking for talks. But Pompey refused. He knew that JC was just trying to stall him and catch him in a battle on Italian soil. And Pompey wasn't about to be caught out…

OR CAUGHT AT ALL, THANK YOU VERY MUCH!

JC reached the port too late to catch Pompey. Leaving his exhausted troops to rest there, he finally travelled to Rome.

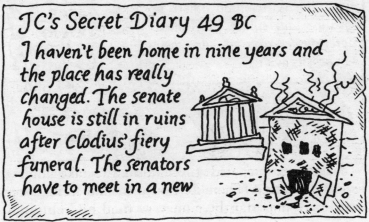

JC's Secret Diary 49 BC

I haven't been home in nine years and the place has really changed. The senate house is still in ruins after Clodius' fiery funeral. The senators have to meet in a new

123

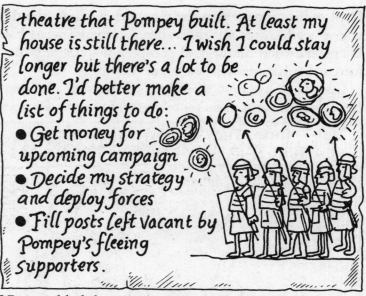

theatre that Pompey built. At least my house is still there... I wish I could stay longer but there's a lot to be done. I'd better make a list of things to do:
- Get money for upcoming campaign
- Decide my strategy and deploy forces
- Fill posts left vacant by Pompey's fleeing supporters.

JC assembled the remaining senators and told them why he was going to war. He tried to set their minds at rest. He told them:

My aim is to outdo others in justice and equity, as I have previously striven to outdo them in achievement.

What he meant was that there would be no slaughter of Roman citizens if he could help it. In Gaul JC had been quite happy to slaughter men, women and children.

124

But when it came to fighting Romans, JC knew that he would need to change. In this war he would be merciful; as the senators captured at Corfinium could testify. (They were still alive and that was proof enough.)

Despite JC's speech, the senate refused to vote him any money. But JC didn't let that stop him…

Having got the gold he needed, JC sent three legions to Africa under the charge of a man called Curio. Then he put Lepidus in charge of Rome and Mark Antony in charge of the rest of Italy. With that, he set out for Spain. Why Spain? Well, Pompey's best troops were there but, with Pompey in Greece, they lacked an overall leader. As Caesar said at the time…

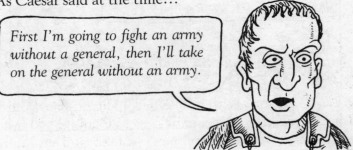

First I'm going to fight an army without a general, then I'll take on the general without an army.

The war in Spain

The campaign in Spain showed what an excellent military commander JC had become. In two months he defeated seven of Pompey's best legions. The campaign was all about moving troops swiftly from place to place, harassing the enemy. This was exactly the kind of campaign that JC had perfected in Gaul. Here are some of the tricks he used to cross a river that stood in his way…

JC's Military Manual

How to Cross a River

I Have troops build British-style coracles made of animal hide and wattle frames.

MADE IN BRITAIN

II Have engineers dig massive channels, draining water away so the river is shallow enough to cross.

WATER LOT OF WORK THIS IS…

III Cross river to victory!

JC soon had the Pompeians surrounded. His officers wanted to attack but JC refused. Instead he set up camp and waited…

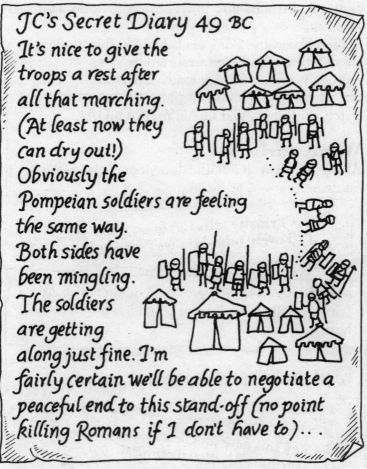

JC's Secret Diary 49 BC

It's nice to give the troops a rest after all that marching. (At least now they can dry out!) Obviously the Pompeian soldiers are feeling the same way. Both sides have been mingling. The soldiers are getting along just fine. I'm fairly certain we'll be able to negotiate a peaceful end to this stand-off (no point killing Romans if I don't have to)…

Sadly, the local Pompeian commander was less relaxed about the situation. Any of JC's men discovered in the wrong camp were killed. In response, JC sent back any

Pompeian soldiers found in *his* camp. Of course JC wouldn't have hesitated to execute the Pompeian troops if he'd needed to. But the message now was clear: JC was civilized and merciful; it was his opponents that were savage killers.

Pretty soon the Pompeians had hardly any support at all and they were forced to surrender.

JC sent some of the enemy soldiers home and spread out others among his own legions. He left four legions to watch over Spain and set out for Rome.

World war!

Along the way JC found out about two setbacks to his cause:

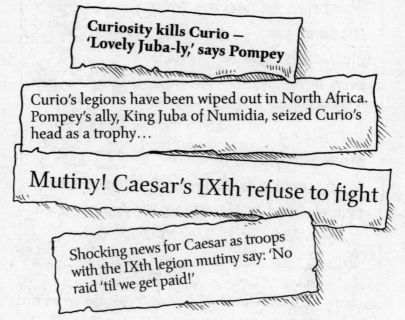

**Curiosity kills Curio —
'Lovely Juba-ly,' says Pompey**

Curio's legions have been wiped out in North Africa. Pompey's ally, King Juba of Numidia, seized Curio's head as a trophy...

Mutiny! Caesar's IXth refuse to fight

Shocking news for Caesar as troops with the IXth legion mutiny say: 'No raid 'til we get paid!'

Africa would have to wait; JC now had to act quickly to bring his remaining troops back onside. He met the mutineers at Placentia on his way back to Rome. He pretended that he was so angry he was going to decimate the legion. (That means he would have one in ten of them executed.) Then he rounded up the 120 worst troublemakers and killed only 12 of them instead...

The 11-day dictator

Back in Rome, JC embarked on a whirlwind political programme...

He accepted the post of dictator.

He held elections for next year's consuls (which his candidates won).

He filled all the vacant posts with allies.

He ordered 12 legions to head for Brundisium.

In recent years Rome's poor had been getting in deep debt. JC passed new laws dealing with the crisis, allowing those in debt to pay back only what they could afford. His new law was popular with the poor, if not with all the moneylenders.

All this was done in just 11 days, then JC abdicated as dictator.

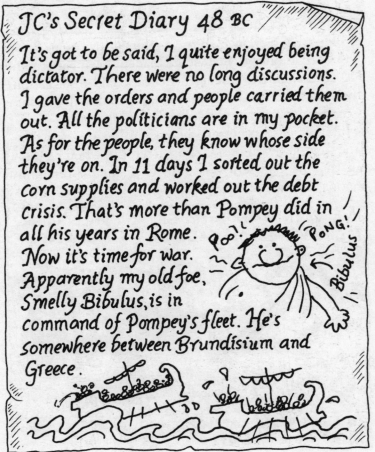

JC's Secret Diary 48 BC

It's got to be said, I quite enjoyed being dictator. There were no long discussions. I gave the orders and people carried them out. All the politicians are in my pocket. As for the people, they know whose side they're on. In 11 days I sorted out the corn supplies and worked out the debt crisis. That's more than Pompey did in all his years in Rome. Now it's time for war. Apparently my old foe, Smelly Bibulus, is in command of Pompey's fleet. He's somewhere between Brundisium and Greece.

Well, it's winter now, so the fool's probably resting in port. He's got a terrible record against me; whenever I come up against him I come up smelling of roses...

JC didn't have enough ships to take all his troops across to Greece in one go. Instead he loaded seven legions and 500 cavalry into whatever boats he could find. Despite the winter weather his men were prepared to follow him; JC really did command the loyalty of his troops.

Bibulus was no better sailor than he was politician. True to form he missed JC's first fleet. But when he found out that JC had sent the ships back for his remaining legions he exacted a terrible revenge...

I'VE BEEN BURNING TO GET MY REVENGE ON CAESAR!

I STILL THINK HE SMELLS OF DUNG.

30 SHIPS WERE CAPTURED AND BURNT, ALONG WITH THEIR CREWS.

Greek manoeuvres

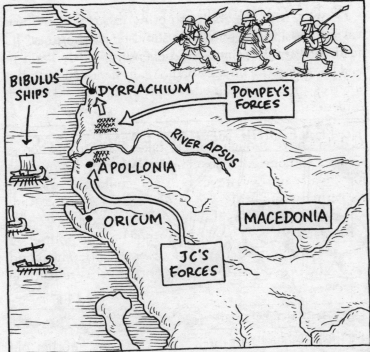

With Bibulus now on alert, Antony had a tough task trying to transport the rest of JC's troops across the Adriatic to Greece. At first JC didn't worry. Within days he'd occupied the cities of Apollonia and Oricum. Next he headed for Dyrrachium. If he could seize the town, Pompey would lose his main stronghold.

In an effort to appear reasonable, JC sent messengers to Pompey asking for peace talks. Pompey rejected the idea of talks and the messengers only succeeded in warning him that JC had arrived. Pompey set out at once for Dyrrachium and reached it just ahead of JC.

The two sides camped on opposite sides of the River Apsus and waited.

Pompey, with his ability to bring in supplies by boat was well positioned for a long stand-off. By contrast, JC needed more troops and was depending on the land to feed the troops he already had. Again he asked for talks, but this time he received a reply from his old friend, Labienus:

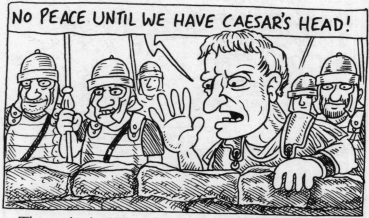

NO PEACE UNTIL WE HAVE CAESAR'S HEAD!

Things looked bad for JC, but this time another old colleague came to the rescue. Worried that JC might trick him again, Bibulus refused to leave his post at sea. Eventually he fell ill and died. Foolishly, Pompey didn't replace him and finally Antony was able to cross with the rest of JC's troops.

The battle began.

JC tried to trap Pompey behind a wall. Meanwhile Pompey tried to ambush JC in a sneak attack. Both sides were desperate to occupy Dyrrachium. At one point Pompey launched a massive bombardment of JC's positions. It almost worked.

JC's Secret Diary 48 BC

Phew! That was close. The soldiers picked up all the arrows that Pompey's archers fired to recycle them; apparently there were 30,000 of them. A soldier called Scaeva came to see me after the battle, he showed me his shield.
'120 holes, Caesar,' he said. 'One for every arrow it stopped.'
I gave him a promotion and a large cash bonus.
Anyone who faces those odds and wins deserves a proper reward. I've doubled the pay and laid on extra rations for everyone else as well. There's a lot of fighting to come and I'll need to keep the lads loyal if I'm going to win.

JC was right to worry about his soldiers. For once their commander was making mistakes. In one battle, JC had to abandon some of his men after a raid went wrong. The captured soldiers were executed by Labienus. Meanwhile Pompey successfully raided JC's defences in the south. Again JC began to run low on supplies. He had to withdraw.

JC's forces retreated into Thessaly. There they hoped to find food.

Pompey was in a great position. He could return to Italy and force JC to invade again. Or he could besiege JC and wear down his rival. But Pompey was under pressure. The officers and the senators who followed him wanted to destroy JC now. But Pompey knew that JC was still a formidable opponent. He refused to be rushed into a fight.

So Pharsalus, so good

The two sides eventually met at Pharsalus on the banks of the Enipeus river. JC arrived first, but it was Pompey who claimed the best position...

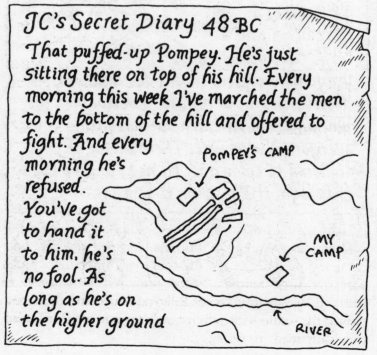

JC's Secret Diary 48 BC
That puffed-up Pompey. He's just sitting there on top of his hill. Every morning this week I've marched the men to the bottom of the hill and offered to fight. And every morning he's refused. You've got to hand it to him. he's no fool. As long as he's on the higher ground

POMPEY'S CAMP

MY CAMP

RIVER

there's no way I can have a go. Charging up that slope would tire my men out before a blow was struck. Still, at least my men are in good spirits. Every day Pompey refuses to fight I tell them it's because he's scared of them. Anyway, the food's running out again and I'm going to have to move off and find more supplies soon. I'll just give Pompey one last chance to fight...

I'M SCARED

POMPEY

SHIVER

KNOLK

Pompey's daily refusal to fight JC was taking its toll on his troops.

IF HE DOESN'T WANT TO FIGHT WHY SHOULD WE?

Just as JC was issuing the order to pack up camp, Pompey moved his soldiers into their battle formation. Both sides were now ready to rumble...

137

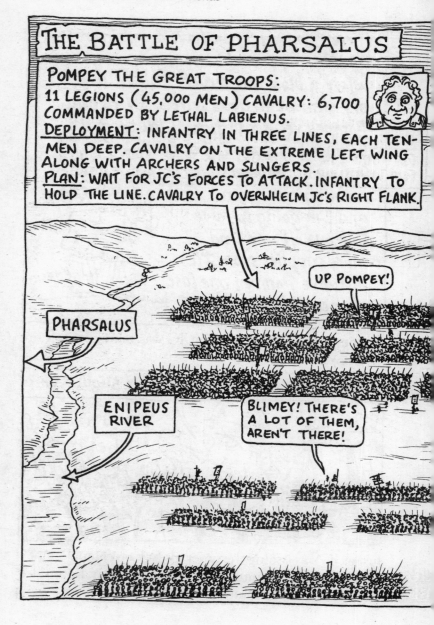

JULIUS CAESAR TROOPS:
8 LEGIONS (22,000 MEN) CAVALRY: 1000
DEPLOYMENT: INFANTRY IN THREE LINES.
EACH SIX-MEN DEEP, CAVALRY ON THE EXTREME
RIGHT WING BACKED BY AROUND 2,000 LEGIONARIES.
PLAN: HIDE 2,000 LEGIONARIES BEHIND CAVALRY.
PUT THIRD LINE OF INFANTRY IN RESERVE. MARCH OTHER
TWO LINES UP TO POMPEY'S FORCES AND ENGAGE.

LABIENUS' CAVALRY

MOUNT DOGAN

JC'S CAVALRY

SORRY ABOUT THAT.

EEUW! I'M LYING IN SOMETHING!

TROOPS HIDING BEHIND CAVALRY

JC took a huge gamble at Pharsalus; he was outnumbered two to one. As two of his infantry lines moved forward JC stationed himself to their right. He knew that if Pompey's cavalry broke through there he would end the day dead, or worse; captured.

Fortunately for JC his former friend, Labienus, had little horse-sense. Instead of attacking in waves he bunched the whole of his cavalry together and rode toward JC. He hoped to smash through using sheer weight of men (and horses).

At first the plan seemed to succeed. JC's feeble cavalry were quickly seen off. But before Labienus could fall on JC's exposed right flank, his horses suddenly ran into 2,000 hidden legionaries with javelins at the ready. The front rank of Labienus' cavalry panicked and tried to retreat, running straight into the horses behind them. In the resulting confusion, JC's legionaries were able to drive the cavalry off.

JC then used flags to order his reserve infantry into the frontline. The enemy suddenly found itself under renewed attack from the front and from their left at the same time. Pretty soon Pompey's soldiers decided the game was up and fled. JC might have had fewer men, but they were commanded by one of the greatest generals in the history of the world. Pompey had more than met his match.

JC's Secret Diary 48 BC

I've seen battlefields before but this time it's different. 6,000 dead Romans is a high price to pay for Pompey's folly. 24,000 soldiers surrendered to me this morning. I've decided to let them join up.

NINE LEGION EAGLES →

I made it clear to them how nice I was being, allowing them to join a winning team. I told my boys that the new guys should be treated with respect.

I'm letting all the officers go (they're mostly from good Roman families, hopefully they'll tell everyone how merciful and just I am). I'm sure they know who's boss now, and can see how misguided they were to follow Pompey. Funnily enough, one of them turns out to be Marcus Brutus, son of my favourite mistress, Servilia. He's a fine lad. It'd be nice to see Servilia and tell her how well the boy

180 MILITARY STANDARDS ↓

24,000 LEGIONARIES ↓

141

did, but I'm not going home quite yet. Pompey's heading for Egypt; I need to find him before he gathers yet another army. Besides, I've been fighting continuously for ten years now. I reckon I could do with a rest. Where better to do nil than in the land of the Nile?

JC sent Antony back to Italy, sent three legions to Asia and embarked for Africa with just two legions of his own. Why so few men? He was Julius Caesar, he'd won the battle of Pharsalus against the odds and become master of the Roman world. Surely there was no one left who would dare challenge him; his reputation alone would be enough to beat his enemies...

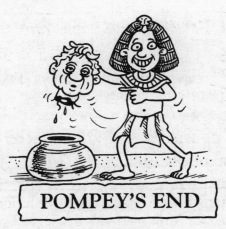

POMPEY'S END

In 48 BC Rome wasn't the only country that was in the middle of a civil war. Egypt was also caught up in a struggle for power. But if you thought the fight between JC and Pompey was complicated, you haven't seen anything yet. In Egypt the two factions were led by a brother and sister. To make matters even more complicated the two weren't just brother and sister, they were also supposed to be immortal gods. It must have made for a very strange childhood...

Cleopatra had not been doing well in the civil war. Her armies had been defeated and her brother was now in charge of the country's main cities.

So, when Pompey sailed into the port of Alexandria, he sent messages to the county's new king, Ptolemy XIII. He asked for the king's protection and was told that the teenager would be happy to guarantee his safety when he came ashore. But Ptolemy had lied…

REPUBLICAN NEWS

48 BC

Obituary: Pompey the Great

Pompey heads into trouble in Egypt

For more than 20 years Gnaeus Pompeius Magnus stood head shoulders above his rivals in Roman life. Now it's just the shoulders.

Having fled the field at Pharsalus, Pompey threw himself on the mercy of the Egyptian ruler, Ptolemy XIII (that's also how old he is). Unfortunately, the Egyptian was as trustworthy as a crocodile's smile. He knew that Pompey was running away from Julius Caesar. In an attempt to get in with Rome's new master, the fearsome Pharaoh ordered his men to stab Pompey in the back (literally) and hack off his head.

WE'LL SEE WHAT JC SPHINX ABOUT THIS.

Rome shocked by death

Pompey wasn't called 'Pompey the Great' for nothing. In politics he dominated the forum in the same way he had dominated military matters (using a well-trained army).

Pompey's death even grated with his biggest enemy. When Julius Caesar arrived a few days later, he met with the teenage tyrant and was presented with Pompey's head and his signet ring. 'It was a really moving sight, as well as being really gross,' said one witness. 'JC actually burst into tears.'

The trouble with sisters

Still, JC decided to stay in Alexandria. One day he received a surprise visit. It's one of history's greatest entrances:

Ptolemy's sister wasn't going to let her younger brother run the kingdom without a fight. She was older than him, more intelligent and far more ambitious. She also happened to be very attractive.

Given JC's reputation as a bit of a womanizer it's not surprising that historians have concentrated on how the Roman fell for this exotic queen. But the truth is that their relationship helped them both get what they wanted…

JC's Secret Diary 48 BC

I must say that Cleopatra's first impression was better than her brother's. (At least she didn't hand me a severed head.) She came on her own (well, apart from the slave). So she wasn't surrounded by a bunch of arrogant advisors. She took quite a gamble, smuggling herself into the heart of the enemy camp; and I must admit I admire that. (Oh, I do have a weakness for the women…)

Frankly, she's much better qualified than her brother to run this country. I don't trust him; he'll stab you in the back as soon as look at you (just ask Pompey).

SNAP SNAP

So that's settled then, I'm going to dump Ptolemy and install Cleo on the throne... It'll be a little Egyptian adventure... All the more glory for me (and for Rome, of course).

The decision was incredibly risky (in fact, most historians think JC behaved rashly because he'd fallen in love with Cleo). JC only had a few thousand men and was in an enemy palace surrounded by enemy forces. Not the sort of place to start a fight. Unless, of course, you were JC...

Ptolemy is over-throne

JC ordered his men to take the boy-king hostage. In response, Ptolemy's forces besieged the palace. The campaign had begun... JC seized the harbour at Alexandria. In the battle, the famous library got badly damaged.

In one battle JC was forced to swim for safety.

Ptolemy's men poisoned the palace water supply with salt water.

Eventually JC released Ptolemy after more of his own men arrived.

Finally Ptolemy was drowned in the Nile after a battle.

Of course, many of Ptolemy's supporters believed he was a god, which meant that he wouldn't be stopped by a trifling matter like drowning. So JC decided to prove that Ptolemy was human. He dragged the body out of the river and put it on display.

JC's Secret Diary 47 BC

I've been missing Rome a lot recently. Egypt has given me a few ideas and I can't wait to get back and try them. It's also given me a new son. That's right;

Cleo's had a kid and has called it Caesarion (she's not that subtle).

Cleo insisted that I take a bit of a holiday after helping her out, so we've been cruising the Nile for the past two months. It's pretty amazing, but I do miss the city. Jupiter knows what they've been up to without me.

I've made up my mind to head home (let's face it I was never one for staying at home and looking after the kids.

As well as leaving Cleo with the new baby, JC also left her some troops and gave her other gifts.

THE ISLAND OF CYPRUS?

IT'S JUST A LITTLE SOMETHING.

Pharnaces the Fool

But JC didn't head straight home, instead he used his remaining troops to defend some Roman territory on the way…

Some of Rome's enemies had tried to take advantage of the war between Pompey and JC. They figured that if the Romans were busy fighting each other they wouldn't be able to defend their colonies. In Armenia, King Pharnaces had murdered the local Romans and made a play for the land.

Pharnaces might have been a great king but he was a useless general. With JC's legions commanding a high hill with a steep ravine below it the king tried what he probably called a 'surprise attack' (his own troops, the Romans and every historian since actually called it 'surprisingly stupid').

Pharnaces' men were ordered to scramble into the ravine, then climb out of it, then climb the hill and then attack the Romans.

When the Romans saw that Pharnaces was serious(-ly thick) they picked up their weapons, waited for the exhausted enemy to finally arrive and then slaughtered them. The battle of Zela was so easy that JC famously remarked…

Veni, vidi, vici.
(I came, I saw, I conquered)

151

A VISIT TO ROME

When JC arrived in Rome, the place was in chaos. As a youth, Mark Antony had gone in for riotous behaviour. As the ruler of Rome, he'd gone in for something similar...

JC's Secret Diary
47 BC Er... I think...

I'm really going to have to Mark Antony down for this. He's a great guy but clearly he's not cut out for leadership yet. I gave him clear instructions: 'Don't make a mess of it', I said. But somehow he's done exactly that.

He's 'forgotten' to hold elections for 47 BC. So there aren't any consuls.

He played around with my new debt

laws, which sparked a riot among the poor. Even the calendar has gone completely loopy; it says it's spring when the weather says it's winter.

I know the last one isn't Antony's fault exactly (the Pontifex Maximus is supposed to be looking after the calendar, but I've been a bit busy, OK?). I'll have to have a spring clean and sort the calendar out once and for all.

Frankly, it's all going to take a while to tidy up.

I'm also going to publish the first instalment of my new book. It's got another great title: 'The Civil War'. I know the war isn't really over but getting my side of the story over will help my cause...

'The Gallic War' is an international bestseller so a sequel could really help my finances as well.

153

But JC didn't have time to sort out all of the mess that Antony had made in Rome. Pompey's supporters were soon causing trouble again.

Hastily JC arranged for himself and Lepidus to be elected consuls for 46 BC. He put Lepidus in charge (sacking Antony in the process). He passed new laws to help poor people who were in debt. Then he turned his mind to war – again.

Never bluff a bluffer

JC knew that there was little time to waste, but his soldiers were desperately tired (ten years of constant warfare will do that). The Xth, the most loyal of his legions, marched into Rome itself. The soldiers knew that JC would need their services in Africa, so they gambled that a threat to leave would force him to raise their pay.

JC listened to their complaints patiently. Then he pretended to agree with them. When he spoke to them he used the term 'citizens', not 'soldiers'. This meant that he'd freed them of any responsibility as soldiers and wouldn't now be asking them to accompany him to Africa, where they could expect to get rich. In effect he'd sacked them. The soldiers realised that JC had called their bluff and clamoured to be allowed to serve under JC again. Graciously he accepted their apology and promised to bring them to Africa.

With one word, JC had stopped a potentially serious mutiny. But he never forgot the betrayal of the Xth. For the rest of the civil war, he made sure they were always in the thick of the fighting.

In the winter of 47–46 BC JC set out once again to face his enemies.

Cato, Labienus and Scipio had joined forces with the African king, Juba, and were rallying their troops in what is now Libya. They'd collected quite a force and were itching to have another go at Caesar.

REPUBLICAN NEWS

46 BC

MEDITERRANEAN

UTICA

LEPTIS

THAPSUS

NUMIDIA

RUSPINA

A bad trip for Caesar?
Julius Caesar's latest campaign got off to a terrible start last week as the great man landed in Africa. Caesar's supporters were shocked to see their leader fall to the ground as he disembarked. It was an ill omen with which to start a campaign but JC recovered magnificently. He kissed the ground and, with arms outspread, shouted: 'Africa, I seize you in both hands!'

JC's luck holds
Despite this bit of quick thinking, JC's position in Africa is risky to say the least. Only 3,000 soldiers and a few cavalry have made it across to Africa; the rest of Caesar's troops are drifting around in the Mediterranean.

Lucky JC

Once again JC was to prove his amazing ability to defy the odds. Here is just some of the amazing luck which saved JC's African adventure…

Soon after arriving in Africa JC found himself surrounded by Labienus' army. Labienus was thrown from his horse and had to be carried from the field. Amazingly the commander left in charge decided to let JC off the hook and wait for Scipio to come and finish the job. JC was able to break out and return to camp at Ruspina.

Once in camp JC was soon surrounded by Scipio's army, with Juba also heading for Ruspina. If the African king arrived JC would be under serious siege. But Juba never turned up; it turned out he needed his troops to put down a rebellion elsewhere. Suddenly Juba also decided to withdraw the troops he'd lent to Scipio.

Scipio and Labienus were still able to stop JC getting food. His soldiers would have starved to death if an entire fleet of merchant ships hadn't happened to sail into the port, laden with corn and supplies.

How not to use war-elephants

JC finally faced Scipio at Thapsus. Juba had lent Scipio 64 war-elephants – truly terrifying beasts used to trample the enemy. JC knew that this would be a mammoth battle and that his battle plan would have to be up to it…

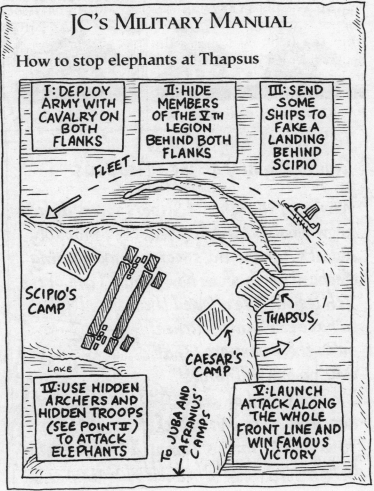

JC's MILITARY MANUAL

How to stop elephants at Thapsus

I: DEPLOY ARMY WITH CAVALRY ON BOTH FLANKS

II: HIDE MEMBERS OF THE Vᵗʰ LEGION BEHIND BOTH FLANKS

III: SEND SOME SHIPS TO FAKE A LANDING BEHIND SCIPIO

FLEET

SCIPIO'S CAMP

LAKE

THAPSUS

CAESAR'S CAMP

IV: USE HIDDEN ARCHERS AND HIDDEN TROOPS (SEE POINT II) TO ATTACK ELEPHANTS

TO JUBA AND AFRANIUS' CAMPS

V: LAUNCH ATTACK ALONG THE WHOLE FRONT LINE AND WIN FAMOUS VICTORY

Once again JC enjoyed some spectacular luck. Scipio's elephants should have trampled JC's troops but the Vth legion drove the elephants from the field and they stampeded through Scipio's soldiers instead...

It was a crushing victory.

JC's Secret Diary June (or is it August?) 46 BC, Thapsus

Who've of thought it? Scipio's forces didn't know what hit them. (Well, they probably did, it's hard to miss scores of marauding elephants!) To show how proud I am of the Vth legion, I've allowed them to have elephants stitched on to their banners. That way no one will forget! I'm not proud of what happened next. We attacked Juba and Afranius' camps. I told the men to be merciful, but their blood was up.

Unfortunately I lost control of them and they butchered the opposition. Such a massacre of Roman citizens is not going to play well back in the forum. Still, I only lost a few dozen soldiers.

Pompey's sons have joined up with Labienus and have run off to Spain. I've sent some troops after them (mainly those troublemakers from the Xth).

I think I'll call in on Cato on my way home. Frankly I'd quite like to gloat over the old goat...

Cato's fate

Cato clearly wasn't keen on a reunion with his old adversary. Before JC arrived, the Optimate leader decided to take matters into his own hands…

REPUBLICAN NEWS

46 BC

Obituary: Cato the Younger

A stomach-churning death

Cato's principled stand against his enemies came to a fitting end this week. Few politicians have the guts to end their career with a flourish, but Cato certainly did.

Knowing that Julius Caesar, his most

fanatical foe, was closing in on his home in North Africa Cato chose a traditional way out. After dinner he sent for a sword and a book. Having read the book he stabbed himself in the stomach. But Cato was a better reader of words than wielder of swords. The blade missed its mark.

Attracted by the sound of his moans, Cato's servants rushed into the room. Seeing that their master was still alive they sent for a surgeon. He tried to stitch up the wound, but Cato pushed him away. With his own hands he clawed at the cut until, at last, he died.

JC wasn't happy. He knew that Cato would now be even more famous (and popular) dead than he had been alive.

The ten-day triumph

When JC arrived in Rome, he had been away for two years. He'd never got to celebrate the Triumphs that he'd been awarded for his many conquests, so this time he made sure the people of Rome had a party to remember…

MY PARTY PLAN

DAY ONE:

- CELEBRATE CONQUEST OF GAUL
- RIDE THROUGH STREETS IN CHARIOT DRAWN BY WHITE HORSES
- PARADE PICTURES OF ALL THE TRIBES I'VE BEATEN
- ALLOW TROOPS TO SHOUT INSULTS AT ME
  (APPARENTLY THIS WILL STOP MY HEAD GETTING TOO BIG)

- SHOW CROWDS THE GALLIC LEADER, VERCINGETORIX (THEN HAVE HIM TAKEN AWAY AND STRANGLED)

ULP!

- CLIMB STEPS IN FORUM ON MY KNEES (TO SHOW HOW HUMBLE I AM)

Veni vidi vici

DAY TWO:

- CELEBRATE VICTORY IN EGYPT
- THE REST, AS ABOVE, BUT NO VERCINGETORIX AND NO CLAMBERING AROUND ON MY KNEES; I'M TOO OLD FOR THAT (AND FAR TOO IMPORTANT!)

DAY THREE:

- CELEBRATE VICTORY OVER PHARNACES IN SIMILAR FASHION

EEK

DAY FOUR:

- CELEBRATE VICTORY OVER JUBA IN JUBA-LATION!

OTHER EVENTS:
GAMES IN HONOUR OF JULIA WITH WILD
BEASTS AND LOTS OF BLOOD.

FIRST-EVER
CAMELOPARD
SEEN IN ROME *

GIVE OUT REWARDS:
20,000 SMALL SILVER COINS
PER LEGIONARY
40,000 SMALL SILVER COINS
PER CENTURION
80,000 SMALL SILVER COINS PER OFFICER
400 SMALL SILVER COINS PLUS OIL AND
CORN FOR EACH FAMILY IN ROME

Lucky I'm loaded!

*This was the first time Romans had seen a giraffe

JC didn't have everything his own way during the
celebrations. On the first day the axle of his chariot
broke. He had to wait for a new one before he could
continue. When he celebrated the victory over Juba, JC
included pictures of the deaths of Scipio and Cato, a rare
mistake from such a skilful politician. The crowds were
pleased to celebrate Roman victories over foreigners, but
when it came to their own citizens it was a different
matter. JC was booed and jeered.

The senate, desperate to keep up with their new boss, commissioned a statue of JC to stand in Rome's main temple. When it was unveiled, there was outrage. The inscription read: 'Julius Divus' or 'Julius the God'. When JC saw the public weren't happy he quietly had it erased.

Clearly the Roman people weren't ready to be ruled by a god just yet.

Despite these problems, the Triumph was a triumph. For ten days Rome partied like it had never partied before...

The date for reform

After that, JC got down to business. The senate (in recognition of the fact that JC was the only man around capable of running the government) appointed him dictator for ten years. Now JC could turn his attention to the reforms that Rome desperately needed.

The trouble with Rome was that it was still run as a city. That was fine, for a city, but by 46 BC Rome wasn't just the city of Rome. It was most of the rest of the known world as well. JC himself had added Gaul and most of Spain to Roman territory. It was no good conquering all these lands and trying to run them using the same old government. So JC began a sweeping programme of reforms, at least one of which we still enjoy today...

I JC increased the number of senators from 600 to 900 (allowing foreigners and soldiers in for the first time).

II To prevent slave uprisings and to ensure that poor citizens could find work, JC made it law that one in three men working the land had to be free (ie not slaves).

III JC settled his veterans on good land; some in Italy, some in Gaul and some in Africa.

IV In an attempt to restrain Rome's extravagant waste, JC banned certain luxury goods.

While pushing through these reforms, JC also pardoned many of the men who'd fought against him in the civil war. Men like Cassius Longinus and Marcus Brutus were even given jobs in JC's government, despite having been followers of Pompey before.

Next JC turned his attention to the Roman calendar.

Forum fact: The Roman calendar. Rome's calendar used 12 months based on the cycle of the moon. Priests put in extra days to keep it in step with the seasons. Sometimes they forgot, with dire consequences.

Instead of having weeks, the Romans divided their months into the kalends (the 1st), the nones (the 7th) and the ides (the 15th). Other days were known by where they sat in relation to these markers.

In Alexandria JC had met an astronomer called Sosigenes. He'd worked out a calendar that was based on the sun instead of the moon.

Each year in the new calendar was to have 365 days, except every fourth year which would have an extra day (sound familiar?). The year would begin on the first of January and each month would switch between 31 and 30 days long, except February which JC said should have

29 days normally and 30 days in a leap year. In recognition of JC's contribution (and as a way of voting him even more honours) the senate named the month of July after him. (This led to a bit of confusion later when Emperor Augustus decided to name a month after himself. Augustus stole a day from February and added it to August so that his month wouldn't be shorter than JC's.)

Finally, to get the calendar back in step with the seasons JC ordered an extra 80 days inserted into 46 BC, making it one of the longest years in history. JC called it 'the last year of confusion'.

Queens and statues

Not everyone welcomed JC's reforms, and soon the rich of Rome had another reason to be scandalized by his behaviour…

Statuesque queen gets statue on state visit

The state visit of Queen Cleopatra was always going to be controversial. Officially this exotic dish is in town to cook up a treaty with Rome. But tongues will wag and some have noted that handsome dictator, Julius Caesar, is in need of a break from his frantic political schedule. What better way to relax than with his regal mistress and their son?

JC has installed Cleo and son in fine style by the river. In honour of her highness he's also commissioned a statue of the royal minx for the forum. This has caused outcry in some quarters. 'Rome's a republic and shouldn't be celebrating kings or queens,' said an upset senator.

It's not known what Calpurnia thinks about this visit. But close friends say she's long been resigned to JC's way with women. 'At least he consorts with queens and nobility, not your riff-raff,' said one.

JC didn't have much time to enjoy Cleopatra's visit. He was far too busy, and not just in Rome...

POMPEY'S BOYS

JC spent a little under a year (admittedly a very *long* year) in Rome before he needed to stretch his legs (or legions) again...

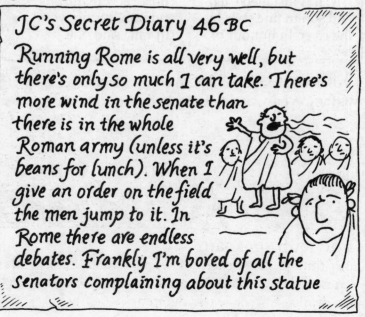

JC's Secret Diary 46 BC

Running Rome is all very well, but there's only so much I can take. There's more wind in the senate than there is in the whole Roman army (unless it's beans for lunch). When I give an order on the field the men jump to it. In Rome there are endless debates. Frankly I'm bored of all the senators complaining about this statue

or that statute. I'm bored of all the parties and feasts and banquets and games.
I need a bit of military action to perk me up...

JC weighed up invading Parthia, where Crassus had come a cropper. But instead he was forced to head for Spain. The troops he had sent to put down the Spanish rebels had failed. Pompey's sons, Sextus and Gnaeus, had met up with Labienus. Between them they had raised 13 legions. They'd seized the city of Cordoba and nearby towns loyal to JC were under siege.

JC didn't hang around. In just 27 days he travelled from Rome to Cordoba (that's almost 1,500 miles). In fact he travelled so fast that his arrival took both his supporters and his opponents by surprise.

HAIL, CAESAR WHERE DID HE HAIL FROM?

The pain in Spain

Last time JC had beaten his opponents in Spain with a series of daring manoeuvres. There had been relatively few deaths. This time was different...

REPUBLICAN NEWS

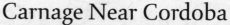

45 BC

Carnage Near Cordoba

Cities across Spain were mourning last week after news spread of recent developments near Cordoba. Siege and counter-siege has resulted in the devastation of several cities. At Ategua the garrison commander, Munatius Plancus, faced a blockade by Julius Caesar's legions. Local inhabitants suggested giving up, so murderous Munatius rounded them up and butchered them. Scores of corpses were thrown over the city wall. After Ategua, JC is on his way to Munda, pursuing Pompey. The pursuit is so hot that several fires have started. Many towns and villages have been burnt.

The two sides finally fought each other at Munda. The Pompeians had around 13 legions. JC had eight, but his forces included a squadron of cavalry commanded by Bogud (a North African king). The Pompeians held the higher ground while JC camped in the plain below.

The enemy had the advantage – so why did JC accept battle?

JC's troops were getting restless. If JC refused to fight, he might lose the confidence of his soldiers. JC's legions were also very experienced. The enemy legions were new and unused to battle. Besides – when did poor odds bother a risk-taker like JC?

The battle began badly for JC. As the advance started JC tried to tighten up his battle lines. The enemy saw the delay and thought that JC didn't want to fight.

As the two sides approached each other, the Pompeians took advantage of the higher ground. They pressed forward and the unthinkable happened. JC's soldiers began to retreat. When he saw this happening JC actually thought about killing himself. But instead he shouted to his men that this was the end of Caesar and the end of their military service. Taking off his helmet (so that everyone could see his face) he plunged into the battle.

JC's presence on the front line turned the battle. The famous Xth broke through and threatened to attack the Pompeian's exposed left side. In response, Labienus moved some men from the front line to meet the threat to the left and JC made good use of the enemy confusion…

In the panic, JC's men routed the enemy. Thirty thousand Pompeian soldiers died at Munda but JC had come close to losing. As he said…

> *At other times I have fought for victory; this time I fought for my life.*

Gnaeus Pompey was caught soon after the battle but his brother, Sextus, continued to cause trouble in Spain for years afterwards.

JC appeared to lose interest in the war in Spain soon after the battle in Munda. In September 45 BC he met up with his sister's grandson, Octavian, and travelled back to Rome.

SOOTHSAYERS, OMENS AND ASSASSINS

Caesar had come a long way since he'd followed his father around in the forum as a boy. He was the wealthiest man alive, he was dubbed 'the father of the country' and his face appeared on coins. The senate appointed him 'dictator for life'. Julius Caesar was king in all but name. In an effort to suck up, senators awarded him more and more elaborate honours...

JC MUST SIT IN A GILDED CHAIR...

...AT GAMES A STATUE OF HIM SHOULD ACCOMPANY THOSE OF THE GODS...

...HE SHOULD HAVE HIS OWN TEMPLE.

The problem was that Rome wasn't supposed to be run by a king...

One Roman historian says that the senators awarded JC these honours to see if he'd ever actually turn them down (he didn't). Perhaps the senators thought that Rome would rebel against him if they saw him sitting on a throne, claiming to be equal to the gods.

JC's increasingly tactless behaviour made the situation worse. He celebrated triumphs for his victories in Spain. One tribune, who refused to stand during the parade, was asked by Caesar if he was trying to restore the republic. Everyone knew that the republic was dead in all but name, but no one liked hearing JC tease them about it.

AND HE DOESN'T EVEN BOTHER TO STAND UP WHEN WE COME TO SEE HIM ANY MORE.

Rumours that JC wanted to become king swept the capital. One prankster put a crown on his statue. When it was discovered in the morning two tribunes made a point of removing it and telling citizens that they'd prosecute anyone calling JC 'King'. JC was furious; he kicked the tribunes out of office, telling them that it would be up to *him* to decide how to deal with the king issue.

Eventually JC decided to take the pulse of the people…

Every February Rome celebrated the festival of Lupercalia. Men would dress is nothing but goatskins. They'd run around and lightly whip any women they found with strips of leather. Roman citizens packed into the forum to join in the fun. It was an ideal place to see if how they would react to the idea of King Caesar…

As the crowds watched the celebrations Mark Antony (dressed in his goatskin loincloth) offered JC a crown.

There was silence. Everyone knew that they were being asked a question by JC and Antony. Should Rome be ruled by a king? Then the crowd groaned, forcing JC to refuse Antony's offer. Antony presented the crown to JC three times and each time the crowd forced him to turn it down. The answer couldn't have been clearer – Rome did not want a king.

Even after JC rejected the crown his enemies put it about that he still wanted to be king. JC's ambition would finally destroy the Republic, they said.

But JC's kingly ambition wasn't the only reason the nobles of Rome began plotting against him. They were upset by his ambition and rudeness, but most of all they hated his politics. The senate was now so full of people from the provinces that nobles were unable to fleece the territories like they used to. Rich landowners had to employ free men as well as slaves, eating into their profits.

AND THIS NEW CALENDAR THINGY WILL NEVER CATCH ON...

March

Frankly, a lot of very rich people in Rome were sick of JC.

The plot thickens

By early 44 BC JC himself knew that some in the senate were turning against him...

JC's Secret Diary 44 BC

Cicero had to wait hours to see me the other day. I didn't mean to be rude; I was just busy. I went round his house to apologize but apparently now he's complaining that I cost too much to feed, what with all my staff.
You just can't win with these guys (especially Cicero).
  Anyway, I'm only going to stay in the

city for another month. It's starting to get me down. I'll set out for Parthia in a few weeks; if I conquer them my greatness will be assured.

The other day the mad old soothsayer, Spurinna, told me to 'beware the ides of March'. For some reason it got to me. Maybe it's because there are rumours that people are planning to kill me. I'm being silly, they'd never harm me, why would they? I've always played fair by them.

Despite these rumours of plots, JC dismissed his bodyguard. He was always on the lookout for a noble gesture and by doing this he appeared to be more in touch with the people, as well as fearless.

Unfortunately, having no fear is not the same thing as having nothing to fear. The plot against JC had been building for months. Cassius had been preparing to approach the influential Marcus Brutus. First Cassius had Cicero write a letter praising the glorious history of the Brutus family (it was another Brutus who had got rid of Rome's last king through a window). Then he had his followers write notes to Marcus Brutus, saying things like 'I wish that the old king-killing-Brutus was alive today' and 'You aren't a true Brutus (like the one who killed the king)!' Finally, having primed his target, Cassius spoke to Brutus and convinced him that JC still wanted to be king.

With Marcus Brutus on board it didn't take long for more nobles to sign up. In the end 60 joined the conspiracy. Here are just a few …

Marcus Brutus: Cato's nephew (and son-in-law). Former follower of Pompey. Pardoned by JC. Noble and patriotic. Worried that JC would become king, thus destroying the Republic for good.

Porcia: daughter of Cato, wife of Brutus. Stabbed herself in the leg to prove she was worthy of joining the plot.

Cassius Longinus:
Commander in Pompey's
fleet. Pardoned by Caesar.
Bitter at JC's power and
disappointed at lack of
promotions.

**Decimus Brutus (distant relation of
Marcus):** Fought under JC in Gaul
and in civil war, commanded JC's
fleet. One of JC's most trusted friends
and advisers. Bitter at JC's power.

Gaius Trebonius: Friend of
Mark Antony and supporter
of the first triumvirate.
Bitter at lack of promotion.

These people should have been queuing up to pat JC
on the back; instead they had very different designs on
JC's body…

Dreams, omens and betrayal

JC announced that he would leave for Parthia on
18 March. Before that the senate would meet at Pompey's
Theatre on March 15th – the ides of March.

Some people like to play up coincidences and prophecies in history. But in the days leading up to the ides of March there were too many weird warnings to ignore…

At dinner on the 14 of March, JC was asked what sort of death he thought would be best. He replied:

> *A quick death is the best.*

That night violent storms struck Rome. In bed JC was awoken when all the doors and windows burst open. Calpurnia was stirring in her sleep and muttering. When she woke up she told him she'd been dreaming…

THAT'S NOT A DREAM, THAT'S A NIGHTMARE!

JC was disturbed by Calpurnia's dream. So he decided to ask the official augurs for some good omens to balance out the bad ones. Several animals were sacrificed and the official augurs sifted through the innards looking for signs.

For once, JC tried to obey the omens instead of his passion for politics. He sent Mark Antony to tell the senators the day's session would be cancelled. Just as Antony was about to leave, another of JC's close friends arrived to accompany him.

Decimus Brutus must have believed the omens even more than JC or Calpurnia. After all, he knew exactly what sort of business his colleagues had planned. So Decimus set about convincing his friend to visit the senate...

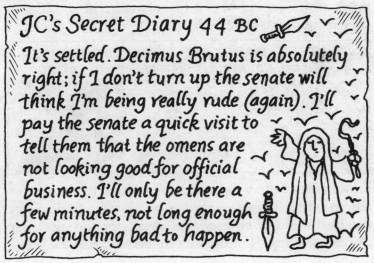

JC's Secret Diary 44 BC

It's settled. Decimus Brutus is absolutely right; if I don't turn up the senate will think I'm being really rude (again). I'll pay the senate a quick visit to tell them that the omens are not looking good for official business. I'll only be there a few minutes, not long enough for anything bad to happen.

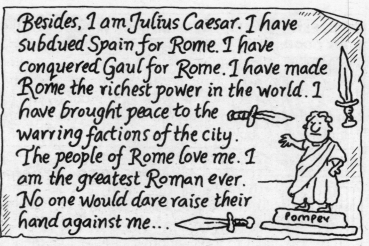

Besides, I am Julius Caesar. I have subdued Spain for Rome. I have conquered Gaul for Rome. I have made Rome the richest power in the world. I have brought peace to the warring factions of the city. The people of Rome love me. I am the greatest Roman ever. No one would dare raise their hand against me...

A trip to the theatre

JC, Mark Antony and the treacherous Decimus Brutus made their way through the busy streets towards Pompey's theatre. JC seems to have been in a good mood. When he met Spurinna he stopped to tease the old soothsayer. After all the ides of March had arrived and JC was still the greatest man alive.

THE IDES OF MARCH ARE HERE AND SO AM I.

YES, BUT THE IDES HAVEN'T PASSED.

Further along the way, another man tried to warn JC of the coming danger. Artemidorus was a philosophy teacher who'd discovered the details of the plot. But instead of telling JC, Artemidorus decided to hand him a scroll. (That's the problem with philosophers, they like writing about the world but rarely like changing it...) The scroll was lost amongst all the other official scrolls. Waiting to greet JC as he arrived at the theatre were dozens of senators, including the conspirators, led by Marcus Brutus. Of course, some of the senators were completely innocent...

The plotters had debated whether or not they should stop at killing JC. Mark Antony and Lepidus were loyal JC supporters. If they were left alive would they seek revenge? But Marcus Brutus had won that argument. He said that killing JC made them look like 'liberators', striking a blow for the Republic. Killing Lepidus and Antony made it look like a common grab for power. And if there was one thing that these conspirators weren't, it was common.

Trebonius distracted Mark Antony on the steps of the theatre, leaving JC to enter the theatre alone, surrounded by his foul friends.

Pompey's foot

The lobby to the theatre was dominated by a huge statue of Pompey. It was here that the plotters struck. Tillius

Cimber grabbed JC's cloak and pulled it from his shoulders. This was the signal for the attack to begin.

First to attack was Publius Casca, but his hand shook, and he only managed to graze JC. In response JC stabbed Casca with his pen, but he was soon surrounded. When he saw Marcus Brutus' sword, Caesar said:

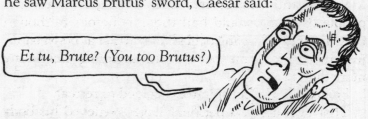

Et tu, Brute? (You too Brutus?)

With that he pulled his cloak over his head and collapsed at the foot of Pompey's statue. The plotters rushed forward to finish the job...

In their frenzy the senators stabbed JC 23 times. (They managed to stab each other a few times as well.) Leaving their victim to bleed to death, the plotters held their bloody daggers aloft and marched out into the streets of Rome.

Brutus and Cassius had been convinced that the people of Rome would hail them as heroes (although they'd employed a gang of gladiators to act as bodyguards, just in case). Some people did celebrate but many more didn't.

Eventually the conspirators decided to retreat.

That evening JC's personal slaves retrieved his body from the theatre. They took it back to the house he'd lived in since his election as Pontifex Maximus all those years ago.

The aftermath

For hours after the murder no one knew who was in control of the streets. It soon became clear that the conspirators didn't have the support of the people (or the legions) to actually take power. So Lepidus moved his own troops into the forum and Mark Antony called a meeting of the senate…

REPUBLICAN NEWS

44 BC

JC dead, killers fled

They might have hoped to make a killing from the murder of JC, but the assassins have since been silenced. Days after they killed the dictator the gang are still laying low. Unable to influence their senatorial friends the plotters were helpless as their future was discussed.

Some senators said that JC should be declared a tyrant. This would clear the conspirators of any crime. But, as Mark Antony argued, if JC was a tyrant then all his laws would lapse. 'Where would that leave all of the people he appointed?' he asked. 'They'd all have to be sacked.'

Oddly enough this argument focused the minds of the sitting

---

senators, many of whom were put there by JC. Faced with new elections and a mutinous mob in the streets the senators decided on a compromise. Mark Antony will bury JC with full state honours and all his laws will stay, but the killers will not be tried for murder.

Mark Antony had caught his enemies in a trap. As JC's body lay in the forum he whipped up the crowd into a terrible fury. He reminded them how JC had filled the treasury of Rome. He detailed JC's many achievements, reminding them that everything he had done he had done for Rome. Finally he read them JC's last will and testament, showing beyond doubt that JC had loved the city of his birth and had been betrayed by people he'd thought of as friends...

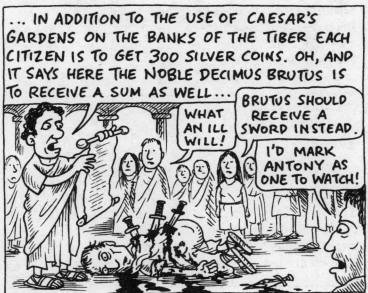

... IN ADDITION TO THE USE OF CAESAR'S GARDENS ON THE BANKS OF THE TIBER EACH CITIZEN IS TO GET 300 SILVER COINS. OH, AND IT SAYS HERE THE NOBLE DECIMUS BRUTUS IS TO RECEIVE A SUM AS WELL...

WHAT AN ILL WILL!

BRUTUS SHOULD RECEIVE A SWORD INSTEAD.

I'D MARK ANTONY AS ONE TO WATCH!

At the end of Antony's speech the crowd's anger burst out. They honoured their fallen hero by burning his body in the forum. Then they went looking for revenge against the murderers. Unfortunately for the poet Helvius Cinna, he shared his second name with one of JC's political enemies. The crowd literally tore him to pieces.

The plotters took the hint. They fled the city – most of them never to return.

EPILOGUE

The men who thought that Caesar's death would bring back the Republic were sorely mistaken. (Most of them ended up pretty sore as well.) Marcus Brutus and Cassius killed themselves in the civil war that followed. Mark Antony fell in love with Cleopatra and then fell out with JC's adopted son, Octavian. The two fought another war, after which Antony and Cleopatra also ended up killing themselves.

Finally, 17 years after the death of his adoptive father, Octavian took the title Emperor Augustus Caesar. The Republic was finally dead. It was replaced by the Empire, which was ruled for the next 600 years by the Caesars.

The emperors that ruled in JC's name were nowhere near as impressive as JC himself. Some conquered more land, or built bigger buildings – one even appointed his horse to the senate, but none had such a thrilling life as Julius Caesar.

His escapades on the battlefields of Europe, in the forum of Rome and in the palaces of the world make him the most famous Roman of all. Two thousand years later generals still read his books to learn about warfare, writers draw inspiration from his life and everyone knows how he met his end at the hands of his foul friends.

All of JC's adventures were undertaken for the glory of Rome. Certainly JC got famous (and rich) on the way, but his main purpose in life was to make his city the world's only superpower. And he certainly managed to do that. It's no surprise then that JC is still at Rome's heart; his tomb is right in the centre of the forum...